Hannah Frey's
Clean Eating
Cookbook

Hannah Frey's

Clean Eating
Cookbook

h.f.ullmann

Contents

Foreword

My parents always stressed the importance of healthy eating and regular exercise, and ever since I can remember, I have been passionate about the subject of health. While I was reading Health Sciences as an undergraduate (with the aim of improving the health of others!), I neglected my own well-being. Suddenly forced to cook for myself, I often resorted to convenience foods. I was so busy with studies and work that exercise rarely formed part of my daily routine. The results were predictable: I became increasingly lethargic, experienced a terrible slump in energy and concentration in the middle of the day, and put on weight.

I soon realized that I had to make some changes. In 2011, I discovered the concept of "clean eating" and from then on completely changed the way I ate. Clean eating has allowed me to find a way of integrating a healthy diet into my everyday life.

It's all about eating natural foods that have been processed as little as possible, foods as Nature made them. Since discovering my love of cooking with natural, fresh produce, I have been sharing my recipes and health tips with an expanding community on my German-language blog *Projekt: Gesund leben (www.projekt-gesund-leben.de)* and various social media platforms.

In this book, I have explained the key aspects of the concept of clean eating and gathered together more than 80 of my favorite recipes from the last few years. It is my goal to reveal how varied, simple, and tasty clean eating can be and that healthy eating and enjoying food are not a contradiction in terms. Most of the recipes can be enjoyed any day of the week and are ready in 30 minutes. I have enjoyed a vegetarian diet for more than ten years and often also eat vegan food, as reflected in the recipes in this book, but clean eating does not also mean needing to exclude fish or meat.

Best wishes, Hannah Frey

Naturally
fresh
simply
good

chapter 1
The **Clean Eating** Concept

For me, clean eating is the key to improved health and well-being; it helps me feel better in my own skin. It combines a healthy and balanced nutritional plan with a modern whole-food diet. The aim is to get away from highly processed, industrially produced foods and back to produce that is as fresh and untreated as possible. Clean eating is all about returning to a natural diet, learning to think about how we deal with food, and listening to our bodies. It will help you discover what your body really needs and what it does not. Clean eating isn't a new idea and certainly isn't a standard "diet" as such. Instead, it's more about making long-term changes to your eating habits and lifestyle. In this chapter, I explain the concept and reveal just how easy it is to apply on a day-to-day basis.

Naturally fresh **simply** good

What is **Clean Eating?**

C lean eating focuses on natural foods. The only way to combat the many harmful environmental factors to which we are exposed is to eat a whole-food diet. The main goal is to make our bodies healthy and efficient and then to keep them that way.

Clean eating is all about untreated, unprocessed foods that are rich in vital nutrients. These include fresh fruit and vegetables, whole grain cereals, nuts, seeds, herbs, grains, shoots, and pulses. Eggs, meat, and fish are not ruled out but tend to take a back seat; essentially, clean eating can be vegetarian, vegan, or omnivorous.

It is important to try to buy food that is seasonal and as local as possible. Another key feature of clean eating is to cook your own food as much as you can so that you really know what you are eating. It cuts out industrially and mass-produced items such as fast food and prepackaged meals, as these contain excessive amounts of fat, sugar, salt, and additives. The word "clean" really means that foods should be "pure" and/or free from additives such as flavor enhancers, colorants, and preservatives (for more information see page 16).

The **Five Basic Rules** of **Clean** Eating

Clean eating is not complicated, and its principles are easy to apply. Here are my five basic rules at a glance:

1. Eat natural foods that have been processed as little as possible.
2. Read the lists of ingredients on food packaging.
3. Eat breakfast every day.
4. Drink 4–5 pints/2–3 three liters of water or tea per day.
5. Eat five small meals every day and keep an eye on the size of your portion.

1. Eat natural foods that have been processed as little as possible

Wherever possible, eat as many natural, unprocessed foods as you can. These will provide you with the perfect balance of vitamins, minerals, trace elements, and dietary fiber. Plan plenty of variety into your menus:

■ Eat plenty of fruit and vegetables, uncooked and raw wherever possible.

■ Choose whole grain cereal products and pulses as a source of vegetable proteins.

■ Use top-quality, healthy fats (cold-pressed, extra-virgin oils) such as olive oil, corn oil, and walnut oil, as well as nuts and avocados.

■ Cook with fresh herbs, and use as little salt as possible.

■ Opt for regional and seasonal foods whenever you can.

■ Avoid foods with "empty" calories, such as white flour and refined white table sugar.

■ Instead of white sugar, choose natural sweeteners like honey, maple syrup, sugar beet molasses, rice syrup, raw cane sugar, coconut sugar, fruit concentrates, or dried fruit. These alternative sweeteners at least contain small amounts of vitamins, minerals, and trace elements that you are unlikely to find in extracted sugar, but even they should be used sparingly. The main aim should be to avoid sugar in all its forms as much as possible. And don't forget that sugar lurks behind terms like glucose, fructose, dextrin, maltodextrin, galactose, and maltose. Steer clear of artificial sweeteners such as aspartame or saccharine, which are simply chemicals.

■ Avoid industrially prepared foods such as fast food and convenience products, which contain not only empty calories but also artificial ingredients (flavor enhancers, colorants and flavoring substances, preservatives, and artificial sweeteners).

■ Eat foods that contain lots of animal fat in moderation; they often have high levels of saturated fatty acids, which can have a negative impact on cholesterol levels. These include chips (crisps), fries, and fatty sausages/meats.

2. Read the Labels, Study the Ingredients

If you are just embarking upon the principles of clean eating, get used to giving the lists of ingredients on food labels a very careful and critical examination when shopping for groceries. Check carefully for the inclusion of additives, flavor enhancers, and food coloring.

Avoid ingredients you don't recognize or can't pronounce. The longer the list of ingredients on the packaging, the more intensively the food has been processed and distanced from its natural state.

Many of the foods that undergo minimal industrial processing still suit the concept of clean eating. These include natural yogurt, cheese, almond milk, and whole wheat pasta, for example. However, you should still read the labels. If the pasta contains only whole grain flour and water, you can eat it without giving it a second thought, even though it has been processed slightly. The same is true for natural and soy yogurt or cheese. You'll discover that some products are clean and some have had sugar added or include additives. One rule of thumb is that any product with more than five ingredients is not going to be clean.

After a while, you'll know which foodstuffs are and are not clean, so you won't need to read the list of ingredients. Remember, too, that the best, one hundred percent clean foods don't need to have a "label" as such, as they contain just one ingredient.

The following example should clarify the difference between industrial products and dishes you cook yourself from clean ingredients. Try to guess the ready meal described by this list of ingredients:

"Tomato powder, vegetable fats (some hydrogenated), modified starch, powdered milk, cooking salt, sugar, flavor enhancers (E621, E627, E631), starch, lactose, whey protein, flour, acidifiers (E330), spices, flavoring."

You will search in vain for vitamins, minerals, or secondary plant substances in this instant tomato soup. The fact that this packet soup actually tastes of tomatoes has very little do with fruit and a lot to do with chemistry. It is no coincidence that dry soup mixes last forever. Why should you eat this mix, with its array of flavor enhancers, when you can make your own tasty and healthy tomato soup from fresh tomatoes, garlic, onions, olive oil, pepper, salt, and a bit of thyme or basil in 20 or 30 minutes?

3. Eat Breakfast Every Day

Our carbohydrate reserves empty overnight and need to be refilled the next morning. A healthy and tasty breakfast gives us what we need for a successful start to the day. The body needs a balanced nutritional resource on which to draw over the next few hours. For many, the idea of a healthy breakfast is impossible due to a lack of time, and of course it's easy to reach for the ready-made muesli mixes, but these generally contain a lot of sugar.

See Chapter 2 for some quick and healthy breakfast alternatives, such as Overnight Oats (page 40) or a tasty breakfast smoothie.

Some people simply can't face the thought of eating first thing, but you really shouldn't starve yourself in the mornings! Studies have shown that going without food early in the day can lead to weight gain, diabetes, and heart or circulatory problems over the long term.

If you don't replenish your energy reserves, you will also start to feel hunger pangs before lunch, increasing the temptation to reach for unhealthy snacks or increase your portions at the midday meal.

Try to enjoy a few moments of peace and quiet at breakfast. The difficulties of daily life can wait for a couple of minutes.

4. Drink Plenty of Water or Tea

Do you often find yourself fighting off a headache or feeling weak and tired? Do you have trouble concentrating? The reason may well be that you are drinking too little. If you don't hydrate sufficiently, you become tired more quickly and may find it hard to focus your thoughts for long. Drinking 4–5 pints/2–3 liters of water or unsweetened tea per day is the ideal goal. Always have a glass of water or a cup of tea at least to hand, and drink a glass of water with every meal. This will increase the volume of liquid you consume per day and help you feel full more quickly. Thirst is often misinterpreted as hunger.

Before breakfast, I often drink a glass of lukewarm water with freshly squeezed lemon juice. After eight hours' sleep our bodies need fluids, and lukewarm water is especially easy to drink, while lemon kick-starts the metabolism.

It should be clear that sugary soft drinks, lemonades, fruit juices, and energy drinks aren't clean; they usually contain lots of sugar or sweeteners.

Alcohol should also be avoided and consumed only on special occasions. It is toxic to our bodies and also contains lots of calories. But don't panic: a glass of beer or wine every now and again is perfectly fine, and you can also drink coffee, within reason. Green teas (especially matcha) contain much more caffeine than coffee, wake you up just as much, and are healthier.

5. Eat Five Small Meals a Day and Monitor Portion Size

It is important to eat regularly and I recommend five meals per day. In addition to the three main meals (breakfast, lunch, and dinner), you can add two small snacks to your food schedule. You probably already graze on the odd nibble between meals, but try to go for healthy foods such as nuts and fruit, or vegetables chopped small to take to work. You'll find some more suggestions on page 72. Consuming small meals more regularly helps to avoid a big insulin rush after eating and keeps hunger pangs at bay, but only you can decide if you prefer to eat three or five times a day.

I prefer the following mealtimes (you can adapt the times to your own daily schedule):
6–7am   breakfast
9–10am   morning snack
12–1pm   lunch
3–4pm   afternoon snack
6–7pm   dinner

However, the size of the portions is as important as the number of meals. According to a Japanese proverb, those who eat only until their stomach is eighty percent full will not need a doctor. And this is correct in terms of the point at which the sense of being full sets in (although only 20 minutes after you have started to eat). So eat in peace, chew your food properly, and enjoy it.

Why Avoid Processed Foods?

Convenience foods have to appeal to a wide range of consumer tastes in order for suppliers to maximize their profit. As a result, salt, sugar, and fat are added to the products as flavor enhancers.

Another consideration is that the foodstuffs used for convenience products are often of poorer quality. White flour (as used in pasta or sliced bread), sugar, hydrogenated fats (as used in potato chips or crisps), and refined oils all have "empty" calories but no fiber, valuable vitamins, minerals, or trace elements.

Convenience products also contain low-cost ingredients; the cheaper the ingredients, the greater the profit, and the base constituents are often treated with pesticides because organically grown ingredients are too expensive.

Preservatives and other additives are added to industrially prepared foods in order to extend their shelf life. These substances often stimulate an excess of dopamine (the "happiness messenger" of the brain), leading to constant hunger pangs. Once you have got used to eating fatty and sweet foods, it can be very difficult to resist the temptation to continue, and the consequences can include becoming overweight and the development of diet-related illnesses. In short, industrial processing destroys nutrients while unhealthy additives are included. Industrially prepared foods can also ruin your digestion, leading to concentration disorders, aggression, rages, and mood swings.

The chemistry in food has further side effects: additives can trigger allergies or cause headaches, nausea, and many other health complaints. The results of eating industrially prepared foods may not become apparent for years.

To see why the foods you eat should be as natural as possible and not industrially prepared, take the hugely popular strawberry yogurt as an example.

This is the list of ingredients from a normal pot of standard strawberry yogurt bought at the supermarket: *"yogurt, mild, 17% strawberry preparation (with strawberries, flavoring, colorant: real cochineal, thickening agent: pectin and guar gum), sugar, glucose-fructose syrup".*

When reading the list of ingredients, one thing becomes clear: strawberry yogurt from the supermarket contains flavoring, colorants, sugar, sugar syrup, and thickening agents. Preservatives may also be included as part of the fruit preparation, but may not need to be mentioned in the list of ingredients in some countries. The pictures of delicious strawberries on the packaging are designed to persuade consumers to purchase the product, but these pictures can often be deceptive. For a yogurt to be described as a "fruit yogurt" in some countries, it has to contain a minimum fruit content of 6 percent. For a 5oz (150g) pot or tub, that amounts to around a third of an ounce (9g), or the equivalent of approximately half a strawberry. Half a strawberry is not enough to provide a taste of the fruit or the typical red coloration of strawberry yogurt, so the food industry looks to artificially manufactured flavorings that are much cheaper than real strawberries.

The yogurt's trademark pink-red color does not usually come from natural strawberries but instead from additive colorants such as beetroot or cochineal, as in the example above.

Cochineal or carmine (a colorant approved as a food additive in Europe with the E number E120) can cause allergies. The same colorant that makes the yogurt so prettily pink is extracted from female scale insects: a strawberry yogurt that includes these is anything but clean.

By contrast, my strawberry yogurt contains exactly two ingredients: strawberries and yogurt. I simply buy both foods, blend to form a puree, and my strawberry yogurt is ready to eat.

That's what clean eating is about!

The **Advantages** of **Clean** Eating

Clean Eating Adapts to your Lifestyle

Clean eating is not a strict diet program. There is no such thing as a system that suits everyone. Different tastes, cultural and ethical backgrounds and convictions, and even physiological considerations, such as allergies and food intolerances, result in a huge range of eating regimes. Nutrition is individual and you need to design a personal eating plan that works for you, based upon the five basic rules (see page 10). Clean eating is not dogmatic: decide for yourself how closely you are going to stick to these rules.

Losing Weight with Clean Eating

Clean eating doesn't mean counting calories or going without. Quite the opposite is true: you can eat more than you used to, you won't be hungry, and you will consume fewer calories at the same time. Clean eating isn't a diet, it is a nutritional method for anyone who wants to stay healthy; the fact that it will help you reach your feel-good weight is an additional benefit. Sport and exercise are also important aspects of the clean eating philosophy, however, and you should work these into your daily routine to boost your sense of well-being.

Feel Good and Prevent Diet-related Illnesses

The best way to help prevent illnesses caused by what you eat, such as tooth decay, digestive disorders, obesity, type 2 diabetes, heart or circulatory conditions, bowel problems, high blood pressure, arteriosclerosis, cancer, and food allergies, and to ensure a good quality of life late into old age, is to stick to a clean diet that provides all the vital nutrients.

However, clean eating can make you feel better now, too, and the following are just some of the positive effects I have experienced myself:

More energy: I feel more energetic on a day-to-day basis, and, importantly, midday slumps, difficulties with concentration, and listlessness are things of the past.

Weight loss: I have lost two pounds (1 kg) with a combination of clean eating and sport, achieving my feel-good weight and feeling better in my own skin.

Strengthened immune system: I am less susceptible to sickness and colds, and even headaches are no longer a problem.

Increased awareness of natural hunger: I am now aware of when I am actually hungry and when my appetite for food is the result of other factors.

Renewed sense of taste: eliminating fast food, sugar, and excess salt means that your taste nerves suddenly become more sensitive; you will enjoy lots of new flavor sensations.

Improved sleep: I find it easier to get out of bed in the mornings, and my sleep is deeper and more restful. My constant tiredness has gone due to my clean diet.

Stronger skin, hair, and nails: my skin tone has improved, and an increased intake of fluids means that my skin is less dry. My hair and nails have also become stronger through my change of diet.

Improved digestion: clean eating, proper hydration, and sport and exercise help digestion.

Clean Eating for **Everyday** Living

Starting the Switchover

Clearing Out your Refrigerator and Pantry

Create an environment in which you will find it easy to eat cleanly and achieve your goals. First, clear out your refrigerator and kitchen cabinets.

Read through the lists of ingredients on all the food labels in your home with a critical eye. Check for additives, flavor enhancers, and food coloring. Any foods that are not clean should be removed or given to friends, work colleagues, or neighbors who may want them—so long as they are aware of why you are giving them away.

Over Time or Overnight?

It is up to you to decide if you want to make a gradual or sudden change. You may need some time to adjust, whatever your existing eating habits. It may be preferable to make changes over a longer period of time—the key is to be sure they are long-lasting. It is also your decision just how cleanly you wish to eat; you can allow yourself deliberate exceptions every now and then. The important thing is that the majority of the food you eat is healthy and helps you to feel fit.

Planning, Purchasing, and Preparation

Plan ahead and half the battle is won: that is the first rule of shopping. Decide in advance what you want to eat and cook, and you will end up buying healthier food, wasting less, and enjoying a more varied diet.

According to one study, for example, seventy-five percent of North Americans don't know in the afternoon what they are going to eat that evening. It is likely that for many people in that situation, the choice will not be a healthy one: a pizza from a delivery service, perhaps, or a can of soup or something similar.

With my stressful job, family, friends, and a household to run, I am often asked how I manage to eat cleanly and resist the temptation to eat takeout, prepackaged, or ready meals. The key to success is planning and preparation. At lunchtime, I don't have to worry about what I am going to eat as I have already prepared my meal and brought it with me to the office. So often I hear excuses like: "I just don't have time to eat healthily." However, this is simply not the case. You can eat healthy food even if you have very little time, you just need to get your priorities right. We are probably all in the same boat; when I get back from work in the evening I am exhausted and not in the mood to spend much time cooking, so I make sure that the main meal takes no more than 30 minutes to cook. Preparing breakfast, snacks, and lunch takes me about 30 minutes, too.

I can hear you saying: "An hour a day? I'll never manage that!" But you can eat cleanly in even less time, and in the following section, I show you how to plan your clean eating week, what to look out for when shopping, and how to prepare your food.

Planning the Week

Plan your shopping ahead. If you set off without a list, you will be easily distracted by what's on offer in the supermarket and could end up with lots of unhealthy items.

Every weekend I make two lists: a weekly plan, on which I write down the meals I plan to cook from Saturday to Friday, and a shopping list. I hang the meal plan for the current week in an obvious place in the kitchen along with the shopping list. If I run out of any basic provisions, I always jot them down immediately, and on Saturdays I add the additional foods I am going to need for the meals I have planned and which I don't have in store. If you find it easier, you can of course plan for only a few days at a time and then go shopping twice a week.

When you are planning, think not just of the main meals but also the snacks you need to take to work, for example. It's also important to make sure the meal plan has plenty of variety; ingredient monotony can result in dietary deficiency symptoms in the long term and will spoil your enjoyment.

As I already have a routine, I need about an hour on Saturdays to plan my meals and do the necessary shopping, but when you begin your clean eating regime, you could just use the recipes in this book for your weekly planning.

Purchasing your Shopping

Here are my four key rules for fuss-free healthy food shopping:
- Never go shopping on an empty stomach. If you hit the stores when hungry, you will end up with mostly sweet and fatty foods in your grocery cart and purchase much more than you intended. Have a small snack beforehand or do your shopping another time.
- Never go shopping without a shopping list. This scrap of paper will help you to buy only what you really need in order to stick to your clean eating plan.
- Always read the list of ingredients when you are shopping and decide if the foods are clean or not.
- Take time out to shop. If you do your weekly shop in a rush during your lunch hour, you will often just grab the first thing that comes to hand, and it will probably be more expensive and less healthy.

Organic or Not?

The basic rule is that the better the quality of the ingredients, the better the dish you will make from them. For clean eating, as many as possible should be grown organically in order to minimize levels of toxins or absorbed substances. Organic foods are generally more expensive than those grown with conventional methods, but I see top-quality foods as a sensible investment in my own health.

Preparation

If you don't wish to (or can't) cook every day, you can prepare ahead or precook your meals. For example, I might sometimes prepare a pumpkin and then freeze it, so I won't have too much more work to do if I fancy turning it into pumpkin soup. Of course, an alternative is to make the pumpkin soup and then freeze it. Vegetables or salad can be washed, chopped, and stored in the refrigerator for the following day. If you like, you can even prepare all the food for the coming week over a couple of days, or a single one. My most useful kitchen assistants are my freezer and the airtight food containers in which I store my food.

Clean Foods

This section features the foods that are essential for a clean diet.

Fruit and Vegetables

These are especially important for clean eating; when freshly harvested, they contain particularly high levels of vitamins, minerals, and dietary fiber. Fruit and vegetables can be eaten raw, in which case their constituent elements are almost entirely preserved. Buy local products for preference: fewer food miles mean fresher fruit and vegetables on your plate. And try to buy mainly seasonal foods, which are both the freshest and also offer the best value. I always have a range of seasonal varieties in the house.

Are dried fruit, frozen goods, and preserves a good alternative to fresh foods?

Dried Fruit
Desiccating (drying out), is one of the oldest methods of preservation. Unfortunately, it greatly reduces the vitamin C content of fruit, as this vitamin is heat-sensitive and water-soluble. Dried fruit is also often treated with sulfur, which destroys vitamin B1, so choose non-sulfur-treated products. Although dried fruit contains fewer vitamins than the fresh variety, it still provides plenty of healthy nutrients, and its high

The Clean Eating Pyramid

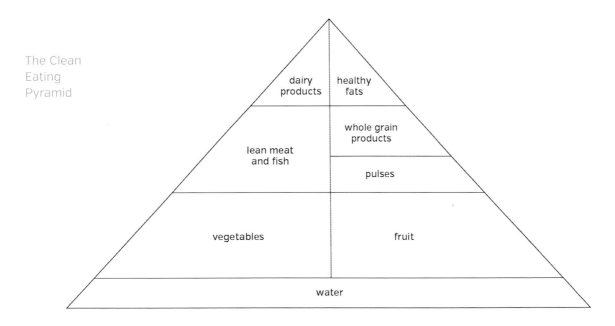

content of dietary fiber is especially good for the digestive tract. If you want to play safe, dry your own fruit in the oven or a food dehydrator. Providing the temperature remains below 108°F/42°C, all the qualities of the raw food will be retained. Dried fruit has a sweet and intense flavor and makes tasty and healthy snacks.

Deep-frozen Fruit and Vegetables

Deep-frozen fruit and vegetables are processed as soon as they are picked, which means that their vitamin content can be higher than produce that is fresh but has been stored for a long period. Deep-freezing is one of the least harmful methods of food preservation, as the vitamins are not destroyed by cold. Fruit and vegetables are usually frozen with no additives, but you should still run an eye over the ingredients list to make sure.

Fruit and Vegetable Preserves

Fruit or vegetables are also processed straight after picking to make preserves. A proportion of the vitamins is destroyed by heat treatment in this case, too, and salt and sugar are often added, so your intake of preserved fruit and vegetables should be restricted as much as possible. Good clean eating options include preserved tomatoes and pulses (kidney beans, lentils, white beans, chickpeas...).

Cereals

Along with fruit and vegetables, whole grain cereals play an essential role in the concept of clean eating. A whole cereal grain contains dietary fiber and minerals in its outer layers (or bran) while the cereal germ is rich in vitamins, minerals, and top-quality protein. The endosperm is made up of starch and protein. Unlike in whole grain (wholemeal) flour, only the endosperm is ground to make refined (white) flour so that it will keep for longer. The bran and germ are sieved out as waste products, so always go for the whole grain version of a cereal, which will also make you feel full much more quickly.

Our modern wheats have come a long way from the ancient seeds that have been cultivated for more than 10,000 years, but old cereal varieties such as spelt, emmer, and Khorasan have been undergoing something of a revival of late. Cereals include the following:

Wheat is our most commonly used cereal.
Rye is rich in B vitamins and minerals.
Spelt is closely related to wheat. Whole spelt grains can be used as a substitute for rice in a risotto, for example.

Khorasan is a cultivar of hard wheat and a so-called "ancient grain" also available as a flour and as flakes. Whole grain (wholemeal) Khorasan flour is lighter than other whole grain flours, which is why I like using it for baking. Khorasan also contains up to 40 percent more proteins than other types of wheat and the proportion of unsaturated fatty acids, amino acids, vitamins, and minerals is higher than with other varieties of wheat.

Emmer is thought to be an ancestor of durum wheat and is an ancient grain just like Khorasan. It is also extremely rich in nutrients, with a very high mineral and iron content, for example, and is far richer in protein than wheat. It also contains high levels of magnesium and zinc.

Barley is the oldest variety of cereal after wheat. Its endosperm is particularly rich in the minerals potassium, calcium, phosphorus, and silicic acid.

Oats are rich in vitamins, minerals, and high-quality proteins, and have a relatively high proportion of beneficial fatty acids.

Millet contains numerous minerals, including magnesium, iron, fluorine, and silicic acid. Millet can be used for risotto, and millet porridge makes a good breakfast. Millet flakes can also be added to muesli or Overnight Oats or Spelt Flakes (page 40).

Rice is one of the oldest known foodstuffs. Choose whole grain rice, hulled rice, brown, red, and black rice in preference to milled and polished white rice, which will have been stripped of most of its nutrients. As is the case with white rice, whole grain rice can be bought parboiled, and this pre-preparation reduces the cooking time to 10 or 15 minutes.

Corn can be cooked in the oven or on the stove when fresh. Dried corn can be ground coarsely (to make semolina) or finely (to make flour). Cornmeal is not very good for baking and is mostly used for polenta.

You can eat grains whole and enjoy the many products made from them, including kibbles, grits, pearl barley, semolina, porridge flakes, whole grain flour and pasta, along with a range of cereal flakes.

I am often asked if couscous, bulgur wheat, and pearl barley are clean. Like pasta, couscous is made from durum wheat semolina (coarsely ground flour), so it is not a variety of cereal in its own right, as is often assumed incorrectly. Instant couscous (a pre-cooked, dried version) is also very popular but is not clean either. However, a whole grain version of couscous is available and this can be used as part of a clean eating program. Bulgur wheat, also made from durum wheat semolina, is not clean, consisting of cooked, hulled, dried, and coarsely kibbled wheat grains. Even pearl barley is not clean; it is hulled and polished grains of barley from which the outer layer (bran) and germ have been removed, just as with bulgur wheat and couscous.

Pseudocereals such as quinoa, amaranth, and buckwheat are not really grains from a botanical point of view and belong to other plant families, but as they have a similar make-up and can be used in similar ways, they are often classified along with cereals. See Pseudocereals (page 103) for more information.

Pulses

Pulses such as beans, peas, and lentils are a key component of any clean eating diet. The plant foods richest in proteins, they also contain lots of minerals, vitamins, and fiber to aid digestion, along with other healthy ingredients. As a result, they also have the advantage of being very filling. However, one disadvantage is the time needed to soak and cook them. This requires careful planning: pulses have to be soaked for at least 7 to 8 hours (ideally 12 hours). Unlike other pulses, lentils require only a short cooking period.

The high protein and fat content of soybeans (soya beans) puts them in a special category and makes them the starting point for many industrially prepared products. Tofu, soy sausage, and soy meat have been industrially processed—sometimes to a considerable degree—and should therefore be avoided wherever possible. If in doubt, have a look at the list of ingredients when making your choice.

Milk, Dairy Products, and Milk Substitutes

Which—and indeed whether—dairy products should be used in clean eating is an extremely subjective question and a matter of considerable debate. Some people only accept raw, unpasteurized milk, as this is completely unprocessed and travels direct from udder to glass. However, it can generally only be bought from a farm. A preferable option is unpasteurized milk that has been subject to constant hygienic monitoring and is available commercially, but this tends to be a rare find in stores. Only pasteurized milk is widely available in most countries, which is not clean strictly speaking, as it has been processed. The same goes for plant milks that substitute dairy products—including almond, soy, and hazelnut milk—unless you have made them yourself.

Only unpasteurized milk and nut milk that you make yourself are really clean in the narrowest sense, which raises the question of how strictly you wish to interpret the concept of clean eating. If you decide processed milk is fine, then the best choice is organic whole milk, and you should try to avoid milk and dairy products with a reduced fat content. If you are a vegan, lactose intolerant, or do not drink cow's milk for other reasons, choose milk substitutes such as almond milk, rice milk, hazelnut milk, and soy milk.

This also applies to cheese, where you are looking for a natural fat content, so steer clear of reduced-fat varieties. Another reason to scrutinize labels and ingredients. Similarly, avoid natural yogurt or yogurt made with milk substitutes such as soy yogurt, to which sugar, flavorings, colorants, preservatives, and thickening agents have been added.

Fish, Meat and Eggs

Fish, meat, and eggs play only a minor role in clean eating and should be consumed only on occasion (no more than once a week). Their consumption is neither expressly recommended nor forbidden; I eat a vegetarian diet (no fish or meat), but it's through personal choice and you must make your own decision. If you eat animal foodstuffs, pay particular attention to their organic quality.

Nuts, Kernels, and Seeds

Nuts, kernels, and seeds contain 35–50 percent fat, the majority of which are different unsaturated fatty acids. These are particularly healthy and have been shown to lower the cholesterol levels of the blood, stabilize blood sugar levels, and prevent cardiac and circulatory conditions. They are also rich in dietary fiber, vitamins, and trace elements.

Nuts, grains, and seeds are an excellent and tasty addition to mueslis, salads, bread, cakes, and cookies. Nut butters can be spread on bread, used to make sauces, or eaten raw as a dip.

Enjoy the variety; the following nuts, kernels and seeds are often in my shopping cart:

Nuts	Kernels	Seeds
walnuts	almonds	chia seeds
hazelnuts	sunflower seeds	flaxseeds
macadamia nuts	pumpkin seeds	psyllium seeds
pecan nuts	pine nuts	poppy seeds
Brazil nuts	pistachios	sesame seeds

Herbs and Spices

If your experience of flavoring to date is salt and pepper, then it's high time you tried out a few more herbs and spices. We consume a great deal of salt, but a tenth of the amount the average person eats would be sufficient. You can get used to things tasting less salty without food being bland. Instead, go for some fresh herbs and dried spices, which lend any dish their own unique flavors.

Herbs are also very healthy. Along with several vitamins and minerals, they contain particularly high quantities of secondary plant substances. Use them as fresh as possible to preserve their valuable active ingredients. The ideal solution is to grow your own herbs in the backyard or garden, on the balcony, or in a flowerpot in the kitchen.

Herbs and spices like basil, dill, marjoram, rosemary, oregano, sage, thyme, chives, parsley, mint, cumin, ginger, nutmeg, and chile pepper will also help you to reduce your salt intake.

Sprouts and Shoots

Growing your own shoots is a very easy way of having valuable nutrients at your disposal all year round. Shoots are real "nutrient bombs" and the essence of clean eating. They are superfoods, stuffed with vitamins, proteins, dietary fiber, and health-promoting secondary plant substances. Enjoy popular options such as cress and mung bean sprouts and classics such as radish or broccoli sprouts. Essentially, all cereal grains, pulses, alfalfa, black and white mustard seeds, fennel seeds, sunflower and pumpkin seeds, and radish seeds are suitable for home growing. Growing instructions can usually be found on the packet label or are included with the sprout germinator.

The important thing is to harvest the shoots at exactly the right time and before the germ uses up its valuable active ingredients in producing further growth.

Fats

Fats have two important functions for the human body: they provide energy and carry fat-soluble vitamins.

There are vegetable fats and animal fats. Vegetable fats include such plant oils as olive, coconut, walnut, peanut, pumpkin seed,

sesame seed, rapeseed, and flaxseed. Avocados and nuts also contain particularly high levels of vegetable fats. The polyunsaturated fatty acids in plants and the oils made from them are especially healthy, raising the level of HDL ["good"] cholesterol in the blood and lowering the LDL ["bad"] cholesterol. This prevents the formation of deposits in the blood vessels and reduces the risk of cardiac and circulatory problems.

A distinction is made between cold-pressed and refined vegetable oils. Cold-pressed oils, which are also known as natural oils, are extracted gently with mechanical pressure but without any use of heat; this means that neither the nutrients nor the flavor is lost, which is why such oils should not be heated too much when preparing food. Cold-pressed oils can be used for salad dressings, for example.

Refined oils, on the other hand, are heated when pressed, and it is during this refining process that vitamins, secondary plant substances, taste, and color are all lost. Strictly speaking, refined oils do not therefore count as clean, but the advantage of the refining process is that the oils can be heated to a high temperature for frying.

I always have cold-pressed olive oil in store, as its high heat stability means it can be heated to anything up to 355°F/180°C, and I also like more exotic oils such as peanut or walnut oil. I use refined oils only sparingly.

Margarine is also a vegetable fat. It is a heavily processed, industrially prepared product, which is why butter is preferable to margarine in clean eating; if you are avoiding animal products, you can use the vegetable alternative. The question of whether butter or margarine is healthier can often degenerate into a battle of conflicting beliefs. Both spreads have their pros and cons and the decision is ultimately one of personal taste and ethical convictions. Whether you go for animal butter or vegetable margarine, use both sparingly and keep an eye on the ingredients.

Animal fats are also found in meat, sausages, milk, eggs, and cheese. These consist primarily of saturated fatty acids, which are considered to be less healthy, so it is better not to eat these foods too often.

Clean Eating on the Go

There is no question that clean eating is easier to do at home, where you have the luxury of preparing your own meals. If you want to be sure that your food is clean when you are out, take it with you from home; I often cook a bit more in the evenings and take it to work with me the next day.

In the Office

Cookies on the conference table, a birthday cake in the office kitchen, or the candy dispenser in the foyer: there are a host of clean eating sins waiting to tempt you at work. It's better to save the deliberate, conscious enjoyment of eating a piece of cake for the celebration of a close friend's birthday than to gulp down a store-bought alternative at your desk. Try to refuse politely but firmly and tame your hunger instead with some healthy snacks (see page 72). And if you do decide on a piece of cake with your colleagues or can't resist a cookie, eat slowly and be aware of enjoying every mouthful.

At the Restaurant

Family gatherings, dinner invitations, business lunches: eating together is an important part of our culture. While dining out used to be a special treat, it's now part of life for many, making it all the more important to select the restaurant wisely and to be careful what you order. There's such a wide selection of tasty, tempting treats that you would resist with ease at home.

Restaurants often serve packet sauces, ready-made dressings, and other prepackaged foods. At the beginning of my clean eating journey, in my wide-eyed innocence I had assumed that everything was freshly prepared in a restaurant, until I had brunch with a friend who told me that my scrambled eggs had been made not with fresh eggs but with powdered egg or some liquid concoction from a carton.

It came as news to me that convenience products are often used in the food industry. Cooking from scratch is a rarity, and we all want our food on the table without having to wait.

Here are some tips on how to manage clean eating in restaurants:
■ Don't let the waiter bring bread to the table. It's so easy to get tempted to help yourself, especially when you're hungry. White bread is generally served with fatty sauces, which are contrary to clean eating.
■ Choose a salad with vinegar and oil or a yogurt-based dressing as an appetizer; American or French dressings, cheese, bacon, and croûtons can quickly turn a salad into a non-clean calorie bomb.
■ Avoid unhealthy sauces and dressings. Fat, sugar, salt, and flavor enhancers make them taste good. Make a point of asking for sauces and dressings to be served on the side, so you can try them and decide if you'd like to add them and in what quantity.
■ Go for whole grain pasta, rice, and pastries, if you choose these items.
■ Avoid alcohol. It increases the appetite and also contains lots of calories.
■ Check out the restaurant ahead on the internet to see what dishes are on the menu. This allows you to decide at your leisure what will fit in best with your clean eating plan.
■ Ask the waitstaff how the food is made and what it contains if you are unable to select the venue.
■ Ask for a tasty fruit salad as a dessert; many restaurants will be happy to oblige.

Parties and Celebrations

Festive occasions, including barbecues, parties, and weddings, tend to take place in spring and summer and offer plenty of opportunities for you to help your hosts by bringing a dish. These could include sushi, crudités, whole grain pizza slices or crackers, vegetable dips, hummus, and yogurt cheese dip. See Appetizers in Chapter 3 for plenty of ideas for perfect dishes for parties (from page 68).

The following tips should help with clean eating at parties:
■ Eat a small snack beforehand in order to reduce the temptation to eat something unhealthy when you get there.
■ Ignore the chips (crisps).
■ If possible, pick a small plate and small portions of the things you'd like to try.
■ Drink plenty of water. This fills the stomach and reduces hunger. Drink as little alcohol as possible.

If you do "lapse," just carry on as normal with your clean eating program the following day. Forgive yourself for your "small slip" and remember why you started your clean eating journey in the first place!

chapter 2
Breakfast

reakfast is the most important meal of the day and you should never skip it to save on calories. Combine complex carbohydrates from whole grain cereals, fruit, and vegetables with protein-rich foods such as (soy) milk and yogurt. I have suggested some healthy breakfast recipes with plenty of variety to give you the best possible start to the day. Homemade muesli mixes and oatmeal make new and interesting additions to the breakfast menu. Even your old favorites become boring at some point. If mornings are really rushed, opt for Overnight Oats or Spelt Flakes (page 40) or smoothies. If you have more time, make some tasty oatmeal or bake your own rolls for a cozy weekend breakfast. All the recipes contain plenty of dietary fiber that will fill you up and get your digestion working.

Naturally
fresh
simply
good

Overnight Spelt Flakes with Strawberries and Pistachios

Serves 2

1⅓ cups/7 oz/
200 g straw-
berries
Scant 1 cup/3 oz/
80 g spelt flakes
1 cup/240 ml
soy milk

■ The evening before you want to eat this for breakfast, wash the strawberries, trim off the base of the stalk with a knife, and cut the strawberries in half. Mix the spelt flakes with the soy milk and then fold in the strawberries. Add the barberries and transfer the mixture to an airtight container or canning jar. Seal and store in the refrigerator overnight.

■ The next morning, pour the spelt flakes into two breakfast bowls and garnish with pistachios.

2 tbsp dried
barberries (or
cranberries)
2 tbsp pistachios
(shelled), to
garnish

"Bircher Style" Overnight Oats

Serves 2

1 apple
Juice of ½ lemon
Scant 1 cup/3 oz/
80 g whole grain
oat flakes
⅓ cup/1 oz/25 g
ground hazelnuts
¾ oz/20 g dried
apple

■ The evening before you plan to enjoy this, wash, core, and quarter the apple. Shred finely and pour the lemon juice over the shredded apple. Fold in the remaining ingredients and transfer the mixture to an airtight container or canning jar. Seal and store overnight in the refrigerator.

■ The next morning, pour the Overnight Oats into two breakfast bowls.

3 tbsp/¾ oz/
20 g raisins
Scant ½ cup/
¾ oz/20 g dried
cranberries
10 tbsp/150 g
(soy) yogurt
Generous ¾ cup/
200 ml (soy) milk

Overnight Oats make the perfect breakfast for those who want to eat healthily but are pressed for time in the mornings. To make them, soak the oat flakes in water and leave in the refrigerator overnight, where they will swell up to the consistency of creamy oatmeal. The basic recipe is very simple: soak ⅔ cup/40 g whole grain oat flakes in ½ cup/120 ml water per portion.

Apple Pie Smoothie

**Serves 2
(about 1 cup/
250 ml each)**

1 apple
½ banana
Scant ¼ cup/
¾ oz/20 g whole
grain oat flakes
½ tsp ground
cinnamon
1⅔ cups/400 ml
almond milk

■ Wash and core the apple and cut into pieces. Peel the banana and cut into small pieces. Blend the fruit with the remaining ingredients in a mixer or form a puree with a hand blender.

■ Serve the smoothie in two large glasses or cups.

Banana Smoothie

**Serves 2
(about 1 cup/
250 ml each)**

1 banana
Dash of lemon
juice
Scant ¼ cup/
¾ oz/20 g whole
grain oat flakes
1¼ cups/300 ml
soy milk

■ Peel the banana and cut into small pieces. Blend in a mixer with the remaining ingredients or form a puree with a hand blender.

■ Serve the smoothie in two large glasses or cups.

I always freeze bananas if they are very ripe and I don't have immediate plans for them. Freezing is also the best method of saving bananas during the hot summer months, when they ripen quickly. Combined with the oat flakes, this wonderful yellow fruit provides a balanced breakfast that keeps you feeling full for a long time.

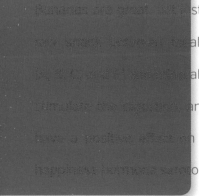

Bananas are great not just in smoothies but also when baked, broiled, grilled, or enjoyed as a tasty raw snack between meals. They are extremely nutritious and healthy, bursting with vitamins A, C, and E and minerals such as potassium and magnesium. High in fiber, they keep you full and stimulate the digestion, and their carbohydrates are a quick source of renewed energy. They even have a positive effect on the brain: the amino acid tryptophan stimulates the production of the happiness hormone serotonin.

Strawberry **Breakfast Smoothie**

**Serves 2
(about 1 cup/
250 ml each)**

1 cup/5½ oz/150 g
strawberries
Scant ½ cup/
1¾ oz/50 g
raspberries
6 tbsp/3½ oz/
100 g (soy) yogurt
Scant ¼ cup/
¾ oz/20 g whole
grain oat flakes
Generous ¾ cup/
200 ml (soy) milk

■ Wash the strawberries, trim off the base of the stalk, and cut in half. Wash the raspberries.

■ Using a blender or hand blender, blend the prepared fruit with the remaining ingredients until smooth. Serve in two large glasses or cups.

If you prefer a more liquid consistency, replace the yogurt with (soy) milk. The oat flakes make this smoothie very filling.

Naturally
fresh
simply
good

Special:
Green **Smoothies**

This raw vegan powerfood is rich in vitamins and makes a great breakfast or fresh and fruity snack between meals. Smoothies can be whipped up in a matter of minutes in a blender, making them ideal for those in a rush. Green smoothies are made with greens, fruit, and liquid, boosted with the superfoods of your choice.

Greens: a simple rule to follow for selecting smoothie vegetables is that they can be wrapped around your finger. Spinach, mint, parsley, green kale, chard, the leafy green tops of carrots, kohlrabi, and red beet, as well as wild herbs, including dandelion, stinging nettles (handle with care), wild garlic, and sorrel, all make perfect ingredients.

Fruit: bananas, dates, and figs in particular take the edge off the slightly bitter taste of the greens. Bananas ensure a smooth texture. Note that red fruit will turn your green smoothie brown.

Liquid: use water, chilled fruit and herb tea, coconut water, plant milk, or juices but not dairy products, which don't belong in a green smoothie.

Superfoods: try matcha tea, fresh ginger, moringa leaves, goji berries, or soaked chia seeds (these will thicken the smoothie). Spices such as cinnamon, vanilla, or cardamom will also add flavor.

Blend until the smoothie has reached your preferred texture. If it is too thick, add a little more liquid.

To help get you started, here are my favorite combinations:
- Leaf spinach, banana, coconut water
- Chard, avocado, honeydew melon, mint, water
- Claytonia or purslane, passion fruit, lime, mint, water
- Green kale, melon, apricot, banana, water (and matcha, if liked)
- Leaf spinach, mango, apple, banana, water

Layered **Apricot** Yogurt

Serves 2

1 unwaxed lemon
1 orange
4–6 fresh apricots
1 pinch vanilla
powder
1 tsp agave syrup
12 whole almonds
Generous
¾ cup/200 g
yogurt
2 tsp edible
flowers [e.g.
elderflower,
sweet violet, or
fruit blossom]
[optional]

■ Grate the lemon zest, then squeeze the lemon and orange.
Wash, pit, and chop the apricots.

■ Bring the lemon juice, orange juice, and lemon zest to a boil
in a pan with the apricots and the vanilla powder. Simmer for
5 minutes, then stir in the agave syrup, and blend the mixture
to a puree.

■ Let the mixture cool. Meanwhile, chop the almonds coarsely
with a knife and mix into the yogurt.

■ Make alternate layers of yogurt and apricot compote in two
glasses or bowls, and decorate with edible flowers, if liked.

Tip

This layered
apricot yogurt
also makes an
excellent
dessert.

Plum Yogurt with Flaxseed Oil

Serves 2

1¼ cups/300 g
soy yogurt
3 tbsp lime juice
2 tbsp flaxseed
oil
6-8 plums

■ Beat the soy yogurt, 2 tbsp of the lime juice, and the flaxseed oil to a cream. Wash and pit the plums and cut into small pieces. Mix the plums with the agave syrup and the remaining lime juice.

■ Arrange the plum mixture in two small bowls or glasses and pour the yogurt over the fruit. Sprinkle with the mixed seeds. Decorate with edible flowers, if liked.

1 tbsp agave
syrup
2 tbsp mixed
seeds
4 edible flowers
(e.g. lavender
or marigold)
(optional)

Flaxseed oil should always be kept in the refrigerator as it will quickly go rancid once opened. It will keep in the refrigerator for 2-3 weeks and can be stored in the freezer for several months, as it has a low melting point.

Crown Rolls

Makes 8 rolls

2 tsp/⅓ oz/
10 g fresh yeast
1 tsp agave syrup
2⅔ cups/400 g
whole grain
spelt flour
Butter or oil,
for greasing
1 tbsp olive oil
1 pinch salt
Seeds, for
sprinkling (flax,
sunflower,
poppy, sesame,
pumpkin,
caraway)

■ The evening before you wish to enjoy these delicious rolls, crumble the yeast and dissolve in 3½ tbsp/50 ml lukewarm water with the agave syrup. Let the mixture rest for 10 minutes; meanwhile, sift the flour and grease a large springform pan.

■ Combine the yeast mixture with the flour, olive oil, salt, and generous ¾ cup/200 ml lukewarm water. Knead the dough—first, using a food processor or the dough hook of your electric mixer, then with your hands—until supple.

■ Divide the dough into 8 pieces and shape these into round rolls. Place one roll in the center of the springform pan and arrange the remaining rolls around it. To ensure they expand to form a crown, the rolls should be touching.

■ Spray the rolls with water and sprinkle the seeds on top. Spray with water again. Cover the springform pan with a lid, plate, or aluminum foil and store in the refrigerator overnight.

■ The next morning, take the springform pan out of the refrigerator and remove the cover. Spray the rolls with water again.

■ Place the springform pan on a wire rack and place on the middle shelf of a cold oven. Heat the oven to 355°F/180°C and bake the rolls for 8 minutes. Now turn the fan on—if your oven has one—and bake them at the same temperature for another 20 minutes. If you don't have a fan oven, increase the temperature to 375°F/190°C.

■ Remove the springform pan from the oven. Let the rolls cool in the pan and then remove.

Red Lentil **Curry** Spread

**Makes about
1 lb/500 g**

½ onion
1 tbsp sunflower
oil
½ cup/100 g
red lentils
Generous ¾ cup/
200 ml coconut
milk (or 13½ oz
can)

■ Peel and finely dice the onion. Heat the sunflower oil in a pan or skillet and gently fry the onion until translucent. Stir in the lentils and the coconut milk. Bring to a boil and then simmer the mixture for 15 minutes, stirring occasionally.

■ Drain off any excess coconut milk, season the lentil mixture with the curry powder, and let cool.

■ Wash, trim, and grate the carrot and stir it into the lentil mixture. Fold in the applesauce, add the lemon juice, salt, and pepper, and blend to a smooth spread.

Curry powder
1 small carrot
Scant ½ cup/
100 g applesauce
1 tbsp lemon
juice
Salt and freshly
ground pepper

Beet Spread

**Makes about
9 oz/250 g**

6 tbsp/50 g
sunflower seeds
1 medium red
beet (beetroot)
1 small onion
1½ tbsp/25 ml
sunflower oil

■ Soak the sunflower seeds in water for 1 hour. Boil the red beet for about 30 minutes. When cool enough to handle, peel the beet and cut into pieces. Peel and finely dice the onion. Heat the sunflower oil and gently fry the onion until translucent. Drain the sunflower seeds.

■ Blend the prepared ingredients with the lemon juice and horseradish to a smooth spread. Season to taste with salt and pepper.

1 tsp lemon juice
½ oz/15 g
freshly shredded
horseradish or
1 tbsp preserved
horseradish
Salt and freshly
ground pepper

The spreads will keep for at least two weeks in a sealed container in the refrigerator. You can also

make a larger amount in advance, but make sure you always remove the spread with a clean spoon.

If you contaminate it with small bread crumbs, for example, mold will soon form.

Mediterranean
Tomato Spread

**Makes about
9 oz/250 g**

1 cup/100 g
sundried
tomatoes
6 tbsp/50 g
sunflower seeds
1 clove of garlic
1 tbsp tomato
paste

■ Soak the sundried tomatoes and the sunflower seeds in water for about 1 hour, then drain well.

■ Peel the clove of garlic and dice finely. Blend the prepared ingredients with the tomato paste, oil, paprika, and basil to a smooth spread. Season to taste with salt and pepper.

4 tbsp olive oil
½ tsp sweet
paprika
1 tsp dried basil
Salt and freshly
ground pepper

Naturally
fresh
simply
good

Special: **Superfoods–**
Healthy Eating **Plus**

Superfoods are bursting with nutrients, which is why they are considered so healthy. They include familiar foods such as blueberries and green kale, but also more exotic products, and I would like to introduce you to some of my favorites.

Chia seeds have high levels of antioxidants and omega-3 fatty acids. These have a positive effect on cholesterol levels and regular consumption can improve blood lipid levels. When soaked, they swell to form a gooey gel that will leave you feeling full for a long time.

Pomegranates contain lots of vitamins and minerals, as well as secondary plant substances. These include so-called polyphenols (more than in any other food) and, thanks to these substances, pomegranates are said to delay aging, reinforce the immune system, and fight infections, among other positive effects.

Green kale makes a tasty accompaniment to hearty meat dishes and is also delicious in green smoothies, baked as kale chips, or simply served raw in a salad. It is rich in vitamins and minerals and its secondary plant substances and antioxidants are thought to offer natural protection against illness.

Matcha is green tea that has been milled to a fine powder from the leaves of the tencha plant. The tea has a stimulating and invigorating effect, making you feel more lively and alert. It is also said to boost the immune system and reduce infection. It has a stronger, more bitter, and more grassy flavor than conventional geen tea.

Breakfast Millet with Crunchy Pistachios and **Vanilla Foam**

Serves 2

½ cup/3½ oz/
100 g millet
1 pinch ground
cinnamon
1 pinch vanilla
powder
1 apple
1 pomegranate
1 orange
¼ cup/20 g
unsalted
pistachios
(unshelled)

■ Bring the millet, cinnamon, and vanilla powder to a boil in 1¼ cups/300 ml water, then simmer over low heat for 10 minutes.

■ Meanwhile, wash and core the apple and cut it into small pieces. Trim off the base of the flower from the top of the pomegranate. Cut it in half and place in a bowl filled with water. Separate out the seeds with your fingers under the water. They will sink to the bottom, while the membranes float to the surface. Drain the seeds through a strainer. Peel the orange and cut into small pieces. Shell the pistachios and chop finely with a knife.

■ Bring the soy milk to a boil and whisk (or foam with a milk frother). Stir the flaxseed oil into the cooked millet. Arrange the millet on two plates and add the fruit and pomegranate seeds. Pour the vanilla foam over the millet and decorate with the pistachio flakes.

1¼ cups/300 ml
vanilla soy milk
(or plain soy milk
and 1 pinch
vanilla powder)
1 tbsp flaxseed
oil

Omelet with **Spinach** and **Mushroom** Filling

Serves 2

1 onion
14 oz/400 g
mushrooms
(e.g. white button
or table)
2 tbsp olive oil
14 oz/400 g leaf
spinach
Freshly ground
pepper
Freshly grated
nutmeg
6 eggs
Salt
½ bunch parsley

■ Peel and finely dice the onion. Wipe any compost off the mushrooms, then trim and slice them. Heat 1 tbsp of the olive oil in a skillet and gently fry the onions and mushrooms. Add the spinach and cook for 5 minutes, stirring occasionally. Season to taste with pepper and nutmeg. Keep the vegetables warm while you finish the recipe.

■ Whisk the eggs, adding a pinch of salt. Wash the parsley and pat it dry, then strip the leaves from the stalks and chop finely. Heat ½ tbsp of the olive oil in a skillet, and make an omelet from half the egg mixture, frying it on both sides. Keep the first omelet warm while you make a second one with the remaining olive oil and egg mixture. Stir the parsley into the spinach and mushroom filling, arrange the omelets on plates, and place the filling on top.

Tip

For a vegan version, omit the eggs and add 14 oz/400 g chopped tofu and 6 tbsp/100 ml soy milk to the vegetables; cook for 5 minutes. Season to taste with salt, pepper, ½ tsp ground turmeric, and 1 tsp black salt (Kala Namak).

Quinoa Granola

**Makes about
7 oz/200 g**

¼ cup/50 g
white quinoa
½ cup/50 g
whole grain oat
flakes
¼ cup/20 g
slivered almonds
3 tbsp/20 g
sunflower seeds
3 tbsp sunflower
oil
3 tbsp agave
syrup
¼ cup/50 g dried
apricots

■ Preheat the fan oven to 320°F/160°C (360°F/180°C for ovens without fans). Place the quinoa in a strainer and rinse under cold running water, until the water runs clear. Drain well. Place the rinsed quinoa, oat flakes, almonds, and sunflower seeds in a bowl. Add the sunflower oil and agave syrup, and mix everything together thoroughly. Line a baking sheet with parchment paper, spread the mixture in a thin layer on the paper, and place the tray on the middle shelf of the oven.

■ Bake for 10–12 minutes, depending on your oven. Check after 10 minutes to see how dark the granola is looking and bake for a few more minutes, if required, until it is pale golden brown.

■ Remove the granola from the oven and let cool completely (it will not harden until it is cool). Cut the dried apricots into small pieces and add to the cooled granola.

Tip

Rinsing washes out most of the bitter substances (saponins) from the quinoa. These can cause food intolerances in small children, so toddlers under the age of two shouldn't eat quinoa.

Gluten-Free Granola
with Coconut and Barberries

**Makes about
7 oz/200 g**

3 tbsp/20 g
sunflower seeds
⅓ cup/50 g
almonds
⅓ cup/50 g
hazelnuts
¼ cup/20 g
shredded
coconut
3 tbsp coconut oil
3 tbsp agave
syrup

■ Preheat the fan oven to 355°F/180°C or 320°F/160°C fan. Whiz the sunflower seeds, almonds, hazelnuts, and shredded coconut briefly in a food processor, or chop finely with a knife. Transfer everything to a bowl. Melt the coconut oil briefly in the micro-wave and add to the mixture, along with the agave syrup. Line a baking sheet with parchment paper, spread the mixture in a thin layer, and place the sheet on the middle shelf of the oven.

■ Bake for 10–12 minutes, depending on your oven. Check after 10 minutes to see how dark the granola is looking and bake for a few more minutes, if required, until it is pale golden brown. Remove the granola from the oven and let cool completely (it will not harden until it is cool). Finally, shell the pistachios and add to the granola along with the barberries.

¼ cup/30 g un-salted pistachios (unshelled)
¼ cup/20 g dried barberries (or cranberries)

Tip

If you want to use dried fruit, add after baking. The granola will keep in an airtight container for at least two weeks.

Exotic Overnight Oats

Serves 2

2 oranges
1 banana
1 cup/80 g whole
grain oat flakes
2 tbsp shredded
coconut
6 fresh apricots
(approx. 8 oz/
240 g in weight,
including pits)
2 tbsp dried
mulberries
Physalis (Cape
gooseberries)
(optional)

■ The evening before you intend to eat these delicious oats for breakfast, squeeze the oranges and peel and slice the banana. Using a blender or hand blender, blend the orange juice and banana to a puree.

■ Add the oat flakes and shredded coconut and place the mixture in an airtight container or a canning jar. Seal and store in the refrigerator overnight.

■ The next morning, wash the apricots, cut in half, remove the pits, and chop into bite-size pieces. Fold the apricots into the Overnight Oats and transfer the mixture to two small bowls. Sprinkle the mulberries over the top and decorate with the physalis, if liked.

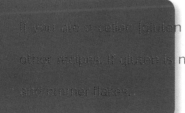

If you are a celiac (gluten intolerant), you can also use buckwheat, soy, or rice flakes in this and other recipes. If gluten is not a problem, you might also like to use spelt, Khorasan wheat (kamut), and einkorn flakes.

Blueberry Muffin **Porridge**

Serves 2

1⅓ cups/7 oz/
200 g blueberries
1 pinch vanilla
powder
Generous ¾ cup/
200 ml almond
milk
1 cup/80 g spelt
flakes
1 pinch ground
cinnamon

■ Bring the blueberries to a boil in a saucepan with 1 tbsp water. Add the vanilla powder and simmer for another 5 minutes, stirring occasionally.

■ Meanwhile, bring the almond milk to a boil in another saucepan. Add the spelt flakes and simmer for 5 minutes, stirring occasionally. Add the cinnamon at the end.

■ Transfer the oatmeal to two breakfast bowls and pour over the blueberry sauce.

Mango Lassi with Cardamom

**Serves 2
(about 1 cup/
250 ml each)**

1 mango
1 cardamom pod
(plus extra, for
sprinkling)
6 tbsp/100 ml
soy milk
Generous ¾ cup/
200 g soy yogurt

■ Peel the mango, slice the flesh away from the seed and cut into pieces. Cut open the cardamom pod, remove the seeds, and grind with a mortar and pestle. Using a blender or hand blender, blend the mango with the cardamom, soy milk, and soy yogurt.

■ Transfer the mango lassi to two large glasses or cups and sprinkle with a little extra ground cardamom, to taste.

Cardamom is particularly common in Arabic and Asian cuisines, although it is mostly used here in holiday season baking. It is related to ginger and is picked by hand, making it one of the most expensive spices, alongside saffron and vanilla. Its essential oils stimulate the digestion.

Apple and Cinnamon Pancakes

Serves 2

2/3 cup/100 g whole grain Khorasan (kamut) flour
1 tsp baking powder
1½ tbsp/20 g raw cane sugar
1 pinch salt

■ Mix the Khorasan flour, baking powder, sugar, salt, and cinnamon together in a bowl. Melt the butter in a saucepan.

■ Beat the rice milk, melted butter, and egg to a foam in a second bowl, then stir it into the flour mixture to form a batter.

■ Wash the apple and cut 4 thin slices across the middle. Carefully remove the seeds with a knife.

■ Heat the oil in a skillet. Place the apple slices in the skillet and spread 2 tbsp batter over each, smoothing down with a spoon. Cook the pancakes until golden brown on both sides. Sprinkle with cinnamon to taste and serve.

½ tsp ground cinnamon (plus extra, for sprinkling)
2 tsp/10 g butter
½ cup/120 ml rice milk
1 egg
1 apple
1 tbsp sunflower oil

Summer
Breakfast Quinoa

Serves 2

½ cup/100 g white quinoa
Generous ¾ cup/200 ml soy milk
Generous 1⅓ cups/7 oz/ 200 g strawberries
Generous ¾ cup/ 200 g soy yogurt

■ Rinse the quinoa thoroughly under cold running water, until the water runs clear. Cook the rinsed quinoa in the soy milk for about 10 minutes, stirring occasionally. Meanwhile, wash and hull the strawberries. Using a blender, food processor, or hand blender, blend the soy yogurt and the strawberries to a smooth puree.

■ Fold the almond paste into the cooked quinoa and mix with the berry yogurt. Wash the mixed berries and, if using strawberries, trim off the stalks. Cut the berries into small pieces.

■ Serve the quinoa mixture in two small bowls or glasses, sprinkled with the berries.

2 tbsp white unsweetened almond paste
Generous 1⅓ cups/7 oz/ 200 g mixed berries (strawberries, red currants, raspberries, blackberries, blueberries, etc.)

Cherry and Chocolate Overnight Spelt Flakes

Serves 2

1 cup/7 oz/200 g cherries
1 cup/80 g spelt flakes

1 cup/240 ml almond milk
1 pinch vanilla powder
2 tsp/10 g cacao nibs

■ The evening before, wash, pit, and halve the cherries. Store in an airtight container in the refrigerator.

■ Mix the spelt flakes with the almond milk in another airtight container or canning jar. Stir in the vanilla powder and the cacao nibs. Seal with a lid and store in the refrigerator overnight.

■ Serve in two breakfast bowls, topped with the halved cherries.

Cacao nibs are ⅟₁₆ to ⅛-inch/2 to 3-mm long splintered cocoa beans. They give the Overnight Spelt Flakes a chocolatey flavor and are also healthy. Unprocessed cocoa beans have high levels of antioxidants and contain the happiness messengers serotonin and dopamine, making this breakfast a perfect start to the day.

Oatmeal with **Quince** and **Gingerbread Sauce** with Crunchy **Pistachios**

Serves 2

1 quince (approx.
7 oz/200 g)
1 tsp lemon juice
1 tsp gingerbread
spice mix
1 cup/250 ml
almond milk
⅛ cup/15 g spelt
flakes
⅛ cup/15 g
emmer flakes
⅛ cup/15 g
Khorasan wheat
(kamut) flakes
3 tbsp/20 g
unsalted pista-
chios (unshelled)

■ Wash and pit the quince, and cut into pieces. Bring ¾ cup/ 200 ml water to a boil in a saucepan. Add the quince and the lemon juice and simmer for 10 minutes. Add the gingerbread spice mix and blend to a smooth puree using a hand blender.

■ Meanwhile, bring the almond milk to a boil in another pan and simmer the three cereal flakes over low heat for 5 minutes, stirring occasionally.

■ Shell the pistachios and briefly whiz in a food processor or chop finely with a knife. Serve the cooked cereal flakes in two small bowls. Pour over the quince and gingerbread sauce and decorate with the crunchy pistachios.

■ As a variation, make this oatmeal with gluten-free flakes (see ingredients on the right).

Variation

1 quince (approx.
7 oz/200 g)
1 tsp lemon juice
1 tsp gingerbread
spice mix
⅛ cup/15 g soy
flakes
⅛ cup/15 g rye
flakes
⅛ cup/15 g buck-
wheat flakes
1 cup/250 ml
almond milk
3 tbsp/20 g
pistachios

Gingerbread spice mix contains cinnamon, anise, cloves, nutmeg, ginger, and cardamom. It is mostly used for holiday season baking, but tastes wonderful in oatmeal, too.

Sunday **Rolls**

Makes 8 rolls

1½ oz/42 g fresh
yeast [2.5 US
portions/
1 European cube]
2⅓ cups/350 g
whole grain spelt
flour [plus extra,
for dusting]
1 cup/150 g
whole grain
rye flour
2 tbsp butter
1½ cups/200 g
sunflower seeds
4 tbsp flaxseeds
1 pinch salt

■ The evening before you plan to enjoy these tasty rolls, crumble the yeast and leave to foam in 7 tbsp/100 ml lukewarm water for 10 minutes. Mix the yeast mixture and remaining ingredients with 1 cup/250 ml lukewarm water and knead for 5 minutes using the dough hook of your electric mixer. Alternatively, use a food processor at the lowest setting, and then knead for another 5 minutes on the medium setting. Cover the dough and let stand overnight at room temperature.

■ The next morning, knock back the dough briefly and divide into 8 pieces. Sprinkle flour onto a counter [work surface] and roll the dough with your hands into thin sausage shapes, each around 12–16 inches/30–40 cm long. Wet your hands and roll the sausages into spirals to form snail shell rolls. Place on a baking sheet lined with parchment paper, cover, and let stand for another 1 hour.

■ Preheat the oven to 450°F/230°C. Place a bowl of hot water in the oven to create steam and bake the rolls in the preheated oven for 20 minutes.

Tip

These rolls require a little more effort to make, but it is certainly worth investing the extra time. They look decorative and are full of flavor.

Blue **Fruit Muesli**
with **Cinnamon**

Serves 2

5 plums
2 blue figs
⅔ cup/3½ oz/
100 g blueberries
1 cup/80 g spelt
flakes
Generous ¾ cup/
200 ml almond
milk
1 pinch ground
cinnamon
2 tbsp whole
almonds

■ Wash the plums, figs, and blueberries. Pit the plums and cut into small pieces. Chop the figs.

■ Mix the fruit with the spelt flakes and transfer to two breakfast bowls. Pour over the almond milk and sprinkle with the ground cinnamon and whole almonds.

chapter 3
Appetizers

Appetizers and starters are the prelude to a meal, its opening chapter. They stimulate interest in the main course. These light and sophisticated ideas for healthy appetizers all adhere to the clean eating principle and will keep the first pangs of hunger at bay, while awakening an appetite for the next course. This colorful mixture of hot and cold appetizers will help you find a suitable starter for every meal. I have included classics with a twist, like the zucchini bruschetta and the meat-free "carpaccio," along with salads, soup, and finger food. Some of the recipes, such as Cucumber Slices with Cranberries (page 71) or Caprese Kebabs (page 88), are also perfect as a tasty, clean eating snack between meals.

Naturally fresh **simply** good

Zucchini Bruschetta

Serves 2

1 zucchini
(courgette)
2 tbsp olive oil
2 tomatoes
1 small onion
2 cloves of garlic
1 bunch basil
Salt and freshly
ground pepper
1 cup/100 g
shredded cheese
(e.g. Gouda,
Emmental, or
vegan shredded
cheese)

■ Preheat the oven to 390°F/200°C or 355°F/180°C fan. Wash the zucchini and cut into slices approx. ⅝ inch/1.5 cm thick. Line a baking sheet with parchment paper, and arrange the slices on top. Brush the slices with olive oil.

■ Wash the tomatoes, cut out the base of the stalks, remove the seeds, and dice the tomato flesh. Peel the onion and the garlic. Dice the onion finely, crush the garlic, and add both to the tomatoes. Wash the basil and pat dry, chop the leaves finely, and add. Season with salt and pepper to taste.

■ Spoon the tomato mixture onto the slices of zucchini and sprinkle with the shredded cheese. Bake in the preheated oven for 10 minutes.

Tip

Bruschetta is an Italian *antipasto* and a popular appetizer. I have used slices of zucchini instead of the traditional toasted white bread to provide an extra dose of vitamins.

Cucumber Slices
with Cranberries

Serves 2

1 cucumber
½ bunch chives,
plus extra, to
garnish (optional)
½ bunch parsley
10 tbsp/5½ oz/
150 g ricotta
1 tsp olive oil
Salt and freshly
ground pepper
1 handful dried
cranberries

■ Wash the cucumber and cut into slices ¾ inch/2 cm thick. Wash the chives and parsley and pat dry. Chop the chives finely, leaving some whole as a garnish. Strip off the leaves from the parsley stalks, and chop finely. Mix the herbs with the ricotta and olive oil. Season to taste with salt and pepper.

■ Arrange the cucumber slices on a serving plate. Spoon the ricotta/herb mixture onto the cucumber, and garnish with the cranberries and whole chives, if liked .

The Canadian cranberry is the big sister of the European lingonberry. This superfruit has gained particular fame for its positive effect on urinary tract infections; its antibacterial properties result from what are known as proanthocyanidins. Cranberry juice is also very popular.

Special:
Healthy Snacks

The clean eating concept allows for two snacks between meals as part of an eating plan. This will keep your blood sugar levels constant, prevent hunger pangs, and maintain your ability to concentrate and function well. The healthy snacks I want to introduce to you here can be packed in sealable containers and taken out with you to work, on walks, etc.

■ Fruit, dried fruit (untreated with sulfur and with no added sugar), frozen grapes, vegetable crudites, cherry tomatoes, preserved vegetables, dried tomatoes. You can also have nut spreads with the fruit, and hummus or other dips with the vegetables.
■ A handful of unsalted nuts, seeds, or trail mix
■ Roast chestnuts or chickpeas
■ Cooked edamame beans (immature soybeans) sprinkled with sea salt
■ Plain or soy yogurt with fruit
■ Rice waffles or sugar-free popcorn
■ Semisweet chocolate with more than 70 percent cocoa
■ A hard-cooked egg
■ Whole grain sandwiches, filled rolls, and filled wraps
■ Homemade snacks such as vegetable muffins, crackers, vegetable chips (made from green kale, yams or Savoy cabbage), sugar-free cookies, protein bars (see page 160), raw pralines (see page 144), chia pudding (see page 152), green smoothies (see page 45), or fruit smoothies (see pages 42–45)
■ Homemade ice cream (fruit chopped up small and frozen with coconut water in ice cream molds, or pureed fruit, frozen)

Organic grocery stores, supermarkets, health food stores, and pharmacies now also stock a wide selection of healthy snacks to eat when you are out and about, but have a careful look at the list of ingredients before you buy.

Warm **Cauliflower Salad** with **Peas** and **Feta**

Serves 2

½ cauliflower
½ cup/50 g peas
(frozen)
5½ oz/150 g feta
½ lemon
½ bunch parsley
½ bunch basil
¼ cup/30 g
mixed seeds
2 tbsp avocado
oil (or olive oil)
Salt and freshly
ground pepper

■ Trim and wash the cauliflower and break up into small florets. Cook the florets in boiling water for 7–10 minutes. Add the peas for the last couple of minutes of the cooking time.

■ Meanwhile, dice the feta finely and juice the lemon. Wash the parsley and basil, pat dry, strip off the leaves, and chop finely. Dry-fry the mixed seeds briefly in a skillet.

■ Drain the cauliflower and peas thoroughly through a colander, then place them in a salad bowl. Add the lemon juice, chopped herbs, mixed seeds, and oil and mix together. Season with salt and pepper. Serve the salad warm.

Stuffed **Giant Mushrooms**

Serves 2

4 large
mushrooms
(e.g. Portobello)
Scant ½ cup/40 g
dried tomatoes
in oil
3½ oz/100 g feta
4 cherry
tomatoes
1 small zucchini
(courgette)
2 sprigs parsley
Salt and freshly
ground pepper
2 tbsp olive oil

■ Wash and trim the mushrooms. Remove the stalks carefully with a knife. These can be used to make vegetable broth (see page 94) or a mushroom sauce (see page 99.)

■ To make the stuffing, cut the dried tomatoes and the feta into pieces. Wash the cherry tomatoes and cut into pieces. Wash the zucchini and shred finely. Wash the parsley, pat dry, strip off the leaves, and chop finely. Mix everything together in a bowl and season to taste with salt and pepper. Preheat the oven to 355°F/180°C or 320°F/160°C fan.

■ Use a teaspoon to stuff the mushrooms with the mixture. Line a Dutch oven or casserole with parchment paper, arrange the stuffed mushrooms on the bottom, and brush them with the olive oil. Place the Dutch oven or casserole in the preheated oven and roast for 15 minutes. To serve, arrange the mushrooms on two plates.

Leaf Spinach
with **Peanut** Sauce

Serves 2

Generous 1 lb/
500 g leaf
spinach
½ onion
1 tbsp sunflower
oil
7 tbsp/100 g
peanut butter
1 tsp lime juice
5 tbsp coconut
milk
1 pinch chili
powder

■ Wash and sort the leaf spinach, then steam it in a steamer for a few minutes, or heat the wet leaves in a saucepan until they wilt (i.e. lose their shape). Drain the spinach thoroughly through a colander.

■ Peel the onion and chop finely. Heat the sunflower oil in a pan and gently fry the onion for about 2 minutes, until translucent. Add the peanut butter, lime juice, and coconut milk and cook the mixture for another 2–3 minutes, stirring constantly until the peanut butter has dissolved. Add the chili powder and season to taste with salt and pepper.

■ Heat 1 tbsp of the peanut oil in a skillet over medium heat and briefly fry the sesame seeds. Transfer the leaf spinach to a bowl and drizzle the remaining 1 tbsp peanut oil on top. Pour over the warm peanut sauce and garnish with the fried sesame seeds.

Salt and freshly
ground pepper
2 tbsp peanut oil
2 tbsp sesame
seeds, to garnish

Stuffed Dates with Walnuts and Roquefort

Serves 2

10 dried dates
3½ oz/100 g
Roquefort (or
other French
blue cheese)
7 tbsp/50 g
walnut kernels
1 tsp olive oil
A little freshly
ground pepper

■ Cut open the dates with a knife and pit. Blend the cheese and walnut kernels in a food processor. Transfer to a bowl and stir in the olive oil and pepper until creamy in texture.

■ Use a teaspoon to fill the pitted dates with the walnut and cheese mixture and arrange on two plates.

Whether you're spending a cozy evening with friends, or are at a family party or a "supper club," these stuffed dates with walnuts and cheese make perfect amuse-bouches. If you have a number of guests coming, the dates can be combined with the Cucumber Slices with Cranberries (see page 71) and the Caprese Kebabs (see page 88) for a colorful finger-food platter.

Tip

If you don't have a powerful food processor, soak the nuts in water overnight in order to make chopping easier.

Vegetable Carpaccio

Serves 2

1 yellow beet
(or red beet)
1 small kohlrabi
1 carrot
¼ cup/50 g
cream cheese
1 tsp honey
1 tbsp olive oil
½ tsp dried
thyme
Salt and freshly
ground pepper
2 tbsp pine nuts,
to garnish

■ Bring a pan of water to a boil and simmer the yellow beet over medium heat for about 45 minutes. Meanwhile, wash, peel, and cut the kohlrabi into thin slices with a mandolin or a grater. Wash, peel, and trim the carrot and slice thinly with a vegetable peeler.

■ Bring another pan of water to a boil and blanch the kohlrabi and carrot slices for 2–3 minutes. Drain the vegetables through a colander and refresh in cold water.

■ Place the cream cheese in a bowl and stir in the honey, olive oil, and dried thyme. Season to taste with salt and pepper. Dry-fry the pine nuts briefly in a skillet until golden brown.

■ When the yellow beet has finished cooking, drain and refresh in cold water, trim off a small section from both ends, and remove the skin with your fingers.

■ Cut the yellow beet into thin slices.

■ Place alternate layers of kohlrabi and yellow beet slices on a serving plate, and top off the tower with the slices of carrot. Spoon the cream cheese onto the tower and garnish with the pine nuts.

Invite your friends round for a "clean dinner" using my suggestion for a perfectly balanced meal.

– Amuse-bouches/cold appetizers: Cucumber Slices with Cranberries, Caprese Kebabs, Stuffed Dates with Walnuts and Roquefort, Vegetable Carpaccio

– Soup: Tomato and Bell Pepper Millet Soup with fresh goat cheese

– Warm appetizers: Pumpkin quinotto, made with zucchini if pumpkins aren't in season

– Main course: Hazelnut Rice wrapped in chard on a vegetable sugo

– Dessert: Coconut and Raspberry dessert (replace with frozen raspberries or seasonal fruits if raspberries are not in season)

Cream of Kohlrabi Soup

1–2 kohlrabi
[generous 1 lb/
500 g, weighed
with skin]
2 cups/500 ml
vegetable broth
[stock]
5 tbsp/75 g sour
cream [or 5 tbsp/
75 ml oat/soy
cream]
½ tsp freshly
grated nutmeg
Salt and freshly
ground pepper

■ Peel the kohlrabi, wash, and cut into pieces. Bring the vegetable broth to a boil in a large saucepan and simmer the kohlrabi over medium heat for 15 minutes.

■ Add the sour cream or oat/soy cream and use a hand blender to blend to a smooth puree. Stir in the nutmeg and season to taste with salt and pepper.

This recipe for cream of vegetable soup is quite simple and can be made with a variety of vegetables [carrots, celery root, or parsnips] and different combinations. If you are really hungry, replace some of the vegetables with potatoes.

Cucumber Salad with Honey, Mustard, and Dill Dressing

Serves 2

1 cucumber
1 red onion
2 tbsp olive oil
1 tsp honey (or
agave syrup)
1 tbsp mustard
2 sprigs dill
Salt and freshly
ground pepper

■ Wash the cucumber and cut into slices. Peel the red onion and slice very finely. Mix the olive oil, honey, and mustard in a bowl. Wash the dill and pat dry, strip the leaves from the stalks, chop, and add to the dressing. Season the dressing with salt and pepper.

■ Place the sliced cucumber and onion in a bowl and stir in the dressing.

Tip

For a vegan variation, use agave syrup instead of honey.

Risotto Balls with
Spinach and Feta

Serves 2

3½ oz/100 g
leaf spinach
¼ cup/50 g
whole grain rice
7 tbsp/100 ml
vegetable broth
(stock)
3½ oz/100 g feta
2 sprigs parsley
1 tbsp whole
wheat bread
crumbs
2 tbsp olive oil

■ Wash and sort the leaf spinach. Cook the whole grain rice in the vegetable broth for about 35 minutes until tender. Add the leaf spinach a few minutes before cooking is completed and stir in. Preheat the oven to 390°F/200°C or 355°F/180°C fan.

■ Press the rice and the leaf spinach through a strainer, squeezing out the excess water. Transfer the rice and spinach mixture to a bowl. Crumble the feta with a fork, and stir into the rice and spinach mixture. Wash the parsley, strip off the leaves, chop finely, and stir into the rice mixture. Finally, stir in the whole wheat bread crumbs.

■ Using your hands, make six patties the size of a table-tennis ball from the rice mixture. Place on a baking sheet lined with parchment paper and brush with olive oil. Bake in a preheated oven for about 15 minutes and serve the rice balls on two plates.

Tomato and Zucchini **Gratin**

Serves 2

2 zucchini
(courgettes),
1 yellow and
1 green
2 large tomatoes
1 onion
5–6 tbsp olive oil
1 clove of garlic
Salt and freshly
ground pepper
2 sprigs thyme

■ Wash and trim the zucchini and tomatoes and cut into slices approx. ½ inch/1 cm thick. Peel the onion and chop finely.

■ Preheat the oven to 390°F/200°C or 355°F/180°C fan. Heat 2 tbsp olive oil in a skillet and gently fry the onion until translucent. Grease 1 large or 2 small Dutch ovens, casseroles, or baking dishes with a little olive oil and layer the zucchini and tomato slices, and the onion, overlapping slightly.

■ Peel and crush the garlic, stir it into 2 tbsp olive oil, season to taste with salt and pepper, and drizzle over the layered zucchini and tomatoes. Rinse and pat dry the thyme, strip the leaves from the stalks, and sprinkle the leaves over the zucchini and tomatoes. Bake the gratin in the preheated oven for 15 minutes.

Fruity **Salad**

Serves 2

7 oz/200 g
arugula (rocket)
½ cucumber
2 small apples
1 tsp lemon juice
7 oz/200 g
cherry tomatoes
1 onion

4 dried dates
1 tbsp orange
juice
1 tbsp mustard
1 tsp honey (or
agave syrup)
1 tsp olive oil
1 pinch pepper

■ Sort, wash, and pat dry the arugula. Wash the cucumber and cut into pieces. Wash and core the apples, slice thinly, and drizzle with the lemon juice.

■ Wash the cherry tomatoes and cut in half. Peel the onion and cut into thin strips. Pit the dates and cut into thin strips.

■ To make the dressing, mix the orange juice, mustard, honey, olive oil, and pepper. Pour the dressing over the salad.

Special: The Building Blocks of Clean **Salads**

A tasty salad makes a perfect and simple main course, especially during the warmer months. The five elements of this building-block system will help you make a different salad combination every day. You will never run out of salad combinations.

The foundation: combine approx. two handfuls of salad greens or lettuce per portion. Dry the washed leaves thoroughly with a salad spinner or let drip dry— the dressing will not coat damp leaves.

The vegetables: choose two or three kinds of vegetables depending on what is in season and allow one or two handfuls per portion.

The extras: spice up the salad with half a handful each of some filling ingredients, including cheese, sundried tomatoes, olives, avocado, or beans (pulses).

The dressing: a top-quality, cold-pressed oil, combined with lemon juice, vinegar (with no added sugar or colorants), or dairy products; alternative vegan versions include soy yogurt or nut spreads. Finish it off with spices and garlic, onions, or shallots. Make enough dressing for several salads and store it in the refrigerator for several days.

The toppings: choose between nuts and kernels, seeds, fresh herbs, or home-grown shoots.

Here are a few suggestions for quick and easy dressings. Just add the ingredients to a sealable jar and shake hard.

Thyme and Mustard Dressing: 2 tbsp olive oil, ½ tsp dried thyme, 1 tsp mustard, 1 tbsp cream cheese, salt, pepper

Lime Vinaigrette: 1 tbsp olive oil, 1 tsp lime juice, 1 tbsp Dijon mustard, ½ shallot (chopped), salt, pepper

Yogurt and Mint Dressing: 2 tbsp yogurt, 2 fresh mint leaves (chopped), 1 tsp lime juice, 1 tsp agave syrup, salt, pepper

Italian Dressing: 2 tbsp olive oil, 1 tsp balsamic vinegar, 1 tsp water, 1 crushed clove of garlic, ½ tsp each of dried basil and oregano

Caprese Kebabs

Serves 2

10 cherry
tomatoes (approx.
5½ oz/150 g)
5 mini mozzarella
balls (approx.
1¾ oz/50 g)
¾ oz/20 g sun-
dried tomatoes
3–4 sprigs basil
1 tbsp olive oil
1 tbsp balsamic
vinegar
Freshly ground
pepper

■ Wash the cherry tomatoes and cut in half. Cut the mini mozzarella balls in half and the sundried tomatoes into small pieces.
Thread ½ cherry tomato, ½ mozzarella ball, 1 piece of sundried
tomato, and a second ½ cherry tomato onto each toothpick.
Make 10 kebabs in the same way.

■ Wash and pat dry the basil, strip off the leaves, and scatter
them over a serving platter. Arrange the kebabs on the basil
leaves, drizzle with olive oil and balsamic vinegar, and sprinkle
with pepper, to taste.

■ For a vegan variation, make the kebabs in the same way
but use avocado instead of the mozzarella: peel and pit the
avocado, cut into 10 pieces, and thread it onto the toothpicks
with the tomatoes instead of the mozzarella.

Variation

10 cherry
tomatoes (approx.
5½ oz/150 g)
½ avocado
¾ oz/20 g sun-
dried tomatoes
3–4 sprigs basil
1 tbsp olive oil
1 tbsp balsamic
vinegar
Freshly ground
pepper

Fried Asparagus with Beans and Tomatoes

Serves 2

3 oz/80 g green
beans
1 bunch green
asparagus
(approx. 1 lb/
500 g)
9 oz/250 g
cherry tomatoes
1 bunch scallions
(spring onions)
1 onion
1 clove of garlic
3 tbsp/25 g pine
nuts

■ Bring a pan of water to a boil. Wash the beans, trim off the
ends, place in the boiling water, and cook for about 10 minutes
until done. Drain through a colander and refresh in cold water.

■ Meanwhile, trim off about ¾–1¼ inch/2–3 cm from the end of
the asparagus spears and peel the bottom third of the stalks if
necessary. Wash the cherry tomatoes and cut in half. Cut the
scallions into rings. Peel the onion and dice finely. Peel and
crush the clove of garlic. Dry-fry the pine nuts in a skillet and
transfer to a plate.

■ Heat the olive oil in the skillet and gently fry the scallions,
onion, and garlic for 1–2 minutes until soft. Add the asparagus,
cherry tomatoes, sundried tomatoes, and the beans, and cook
for about 5 minutes, stirring occasionally. Season to taste with
salt and pepper.

■ Wash the salad greens, pat dry, and scatter on two plates.
Arrange the vegetables on top and garnish with the cress.

1 tbsp olive oil
1½ oz/40 g sun-
dried tomatoes
Salt and freshly
ground pepper
2 handfuls mixed
salad greens
(leaves)
1 handful cress,
to garnish

chapter 4
Entrées and
Main Courses

The main courses selected here are just as delicious whether served alone or as part of a menu. There's something for everyone, and the recipes are sure to fill you up. All the entrées are vegetarian and many are vegan. They are also clean, easy to digest, and naturally tasty, just as a healthy lunch or dinner should be. If you come home after a stressful day or you're short of time at midday, you need a healthy meal that is quick to make, tastes amazing, and won't make your stomach feel heavy. Most of these dishes are easy to tranport, so you can prepare your meals at your leisure and take them to work in a container. You can eat clean on the go and still be sure you are getting all the energy and nutrients you need.

Naturally
fresh
simply
good

Vietnamese-Style Summer Rolls with Mango and Peanut Sauces

Serves 2

½ red beet
3½ oz/100 g
rice noodles
2 carrots
½ cucumber
6 sheets rice
paper

**For the
peanut sauce**
1 small onion
1 tbsp peanut oil
7 tbsp/100 g
peanut butter
1 tsp lime juice
5 tbsp coconut
milk
1 pinch chili
powder
Salt and freshly
ground pepper

**For the
mango sauce**
½ mango (approx.
6 oz/150 g)
2 tbsp white
balsamic vinegar
1 tbsp olive oil
1 tbsp lime juice
1 pinch salt
1 pinch greshly
ground pepper
½ tsp ground
cinnamon

■ Bring a pan of water to a boil and simmer the unpeeled red beet over medium heat for about 30 minutes.

■ Meanwhile: to make the peanut sauce, peel the onion and chop finely. Heat the peanut oil in a pan and gently fry the onion for 1–2 mintues, until translucent. Add the peanut butter, lime juice, and coconut milk. Cook for another 2–3 minutes, stirring continuously until the peanut butter has dissolved. Add the chili powder and season to taste with salt and pepper.

■ To make the mango sauce, trim the the mango flesh away from the seed, peel, and cut into pieces. Use a blender or hand blender to blend the mango pieces with the remaining sauce ingredients to a puree.

■ Cook the rice noodles in water, following the directions on the package.

■ Wash and trim the carrots and the cucumber, peel if required, and cut into thin sticks.

■ Once the beet is cooked, drain through a colander and refresh in cold water. Trim at both ends and remove the skin by hand (you may want to use gloves as the beet will stain everything). Cut into thin sticks.

■ Heat a large pan of water to about 104°F/40°C. Place the sheets of rice paper in the water one by one and lift out as soon as they become soft and pliable. Lay the sheets on a damp paper towel.

■ Place some rice noodles and vegetable sticks in the center of each sheet, leaving enough space at the sides and at the top and bottom. Fold the long sides of the rice paper tightly over the filling and tuck in the top and bottom edges. Serve the summer rolls with the mango sauce and peanut sauce.

Rice paper is made from rice flour and water, so this almost transparent material is especially suitable for people with allergies as it contains no gluten, eggs, or milk protein. It is also low in fat and calories. You can buy it in Asian stores and well-stocked grocery stores or supermarkets. These summer rolls are full of vitamins and low in fat, so are a healthy and tasty alternative to deep-fried spring rolls. You can vary the filling each time you make them and they are extremely suitable as food on the go.

Basic Recipe
Vegetable Broth

**Makes about
1.2 quart/1.2 l**

1 onion
1 clove of garlic
2 parsnips
2 carrots
½ celery root
(celeriac)
5 mushrooms
1 bulb fennel
1 tomato
2 tbsp olive oil
1 dried bay leaf
4 black
peppercorns
1 tbsp dried
thyme
1 tbsp dried
rosemary

■ Peel and dice the onion and garlic. Trim and peel the parsnips, carrots, and celery root. Wash and trim the mushrooms, fennel, and tomato. Dice all the vegetables and tomato.

■ Heat the olive oil in a large pan and fry the vegetables and tomato for 2 minutes. Add the bay leaf, black peppercorns, and herbs and deglaze with 2 quarts/2 l water. Bring back to a boil then simmer at low heat for 50 minutes to an hour. Strain the vegetable broth through a strainer.

■ This vegetable broth will keep for about 3 days in the refrigerator and for about 6 months in the freezer. Larger portions can be frozen in a freezer bag, although ice trays are better for small portions.

■ Alternatively, store the broth for about 3 months in canning jars. To do this, sterilize 14-oz/400-ml canning jars with boiling water and fill with the boiling broth. Seal with sterilized lids, turn the jars upside down on a dish towel, and let stand for 5 minutes. Turn the jars the right way up, let cool completely, and store in the refrigerator.

Many of my main courses use vegetable broth as their base. As most of the concentrates or stock cubes and powders you can buy in the stores contain lots of salt, along with fat and flavor enhancers, they are far from clean; a homemade vegetable broth is easy to make, with nothing more than fresh vegetables, spices, and water.

Hazelnut Rice wrapped in Chard on a **Vegetable Sugo**

Serves 2

2 cups/500 ml
vegetable broth
(stock)

1/2 cup/100 g
whole grain rice

6 chard leaves

1/2 bunch parsley

1/3 cup/40 g
hazelnuts

1/2 cup/100 g
cream cheese

Salt and freshly
ground pepper

2 tomatoes

1/2 red bell pepper

1/2 eggplant
(aubergine)

1 onion

1 tbsp olive oil

1 tbsp tomato
paste

Oregano, to
garnish

■ Bring 1 cup/250 ml vegetable broth to a boil and cook the rice in it, following the directions on the package. Wash the chard leaves, trim off the stalks, and blanch in boiling water for about 1 minute, then refresh in a bowl of cold water for 10 seconds. Let drain on paper towels or a clean dish towel.

■ Wash the parsley, strip off the leaves, pat dry, and chop finely. Chop the hazelnuts finely. Mix both into the cream cheese and season to taste with salt and pepper.

■ To make the sugo, wash and trim the tomatoes, bell pepper, and eggplant. Remove the seeds from the bell pepper. Cut all the vegetables and tomatoes into pieces. Peel the onion and dice finely. Heat the olive oil in a pan and gently fry the onion until translucent. Add the vegetables and tomatoes and deglaze with the remaining vegetable broth. Stir in the tomato paste and simmer for 10 minutes.

■ Strain the cooked rice and drain well. Stir this into the cream cheese mixture. Arrange the chard leaves in rows on the counter and place 1 heaping tbsp of the rice mixture in the middle of each leaf. Fold in the long edges of the leaves and roll up the parcels from bottom to top, fixing in place with a toothpick. Pour the vegetable sugo onto two plates and arrange the little chard rolls on top. Serve garnished with oregano.

Tomato, Bell Pepper, and Millet Soup with Goat Cheese

Serves 2

9 oz/250 g
bell peppers
14 oz/400 g
tomatoes
1 onion
1 clove of garlic
1 tbsp olive oil
Generous
¾ cup/200 ml
vegetable broth
(stock)
4 tbsp millet
5½ oz/150 g
fresh goat
cheese
Salt and freshly
ground pepper
Chili powder

1 tsp dried thyme
1 tsp dried basil
1 tsp dried
oregano
Dried thyme and
dried red pepper
(chili) flakes, to
garnish

■ Wash the bell peppers, cut in half, and remove the seeds. Arrange skin-side up in rows on a baking sheet. Set the oven broiler (grill) to high and broil (grill) the bell peppers until the skin is black and starting to blister. Cover the bell peppers with a damp paper towel, let cool, and remove the skins.

■ Cut out the base of the stalks from the tomatoes and cut into small pieces.

■ Peel the onion and chop finely, peel and crush the clove of garlic, and cut the roasted bell pepper into small pieces.

■ Heat the olive oil in a pan and gently fry the onion and garlic until translucent. Add the tomatoes and the roasted bell peppers. Deglaze with the vegetable broth and add the millet. Simmer everything for 10 minutes and then blend to a puree with a hand blender.

■ Add the fresh goat cheese and season with salt, pepper and chili powder, to taste, and the herbs. Transfer the soup to two plates and serve sprinkled with dried thyme and dried red pepper flakes.

This soup will also be extremely tasty without the fresh goat cheese for those wanting to make a vegan version. Removing the skin from the bell peppers is a relatively boring chore, but roasting intensifies the taste and lends it a slightly smoky flavor. You can skin a large batch at the same time and use it for other dishes over the next few days—such as Millet Salad with Lemon and Mustard Dressing (page 98).

Millet Salad with Lemon and Mustard Dressing

Serves 2

9 oz/250 g
bell peppers
1¼ cups/120 g
millet
2 cups/500 ml
vegetable broth
(stock)
½ cucumber
½ bunch parsley
½ unwaxed
lemon
1 clove of garlic
2 tsp mustard
2 tbsp olive oil
1 pinch chili
powder
Salt and freshly
ground pepper

■ Wash and clean the bell peppers, cut in half, and remove the seeds.

■ Arrange skin-side up in rows on a baking tray and set the oven broiler (grill) to high. Broil (grill) the bell peppers until the skin is black and starting to blister, then cover with a damp paper towel, let cool, and remove the skins.

■ Cook the millet in the vegetable broth, following the directions on the package. Wash the cucumber, peel (optional), and cut into bite-size pieces. Cut the bell pepper into pieces. Wash the parsley, strip off the leaves, and chop coarsely.

■ Fluff the millet with a fork, transfer to a salad bowl, and let cool a little. Fold the cucumber, bell pepper, and parsley into the millet.

■ Wash the unwaxed lemon and grate the zest, then squeeze the juice. Peel and crush the clove of garlic. Mix the lemon zest with the lemon juice, garlic, mustard, olive oil, chili powder, and salt and pepper to taste to make a dressing. Stir the lemon and mustard dressing into the millet salad.

This millet salad is a really handy dish to eat on the hoof. If you are planning to eat it at lunchtime, you can make it the evening before. Add the parsley the following day and it's good to go.

Whole Grain **Spelt Pasta** with Mushrooms and **Pesto**

Serves 2

For the wild garlic pesto
½ bunch wild garlic (ramsons)
1 tbsp pine nuts
1 tbsp freshly shredded Parmesan
1½ tbsp olive oil
Salt and freshly ground pepper

■ Wash the wild garlic, trim off the stalks and leaves, and chop finely. Using a blender or hand blender, whiz the leaves with the pine nuts, Parmesan, olive oil, and salt and pepper to taste to make a paste.

■ Wipe the mushrooms and cut into slices. Peel the onion and chop finely. Cook the pasta in plenty of water, according to the directions on the package, until al dente.

■ Heat the olive oil in a skillet and gently fry the onion until translucent. Add the mushrooms and cook for 2–3 minutes, stirring frequently, then deglaze with the cream. Simmer for 5 minutes over low heat before seasoning to taste with salt and pepper.

■ Drain the pasta well. Transfer to two plates, adding the mushroom sauce and the wild garlic pesto.

For the pasta and the sauce
9 oz/250 g mushrooms
1 onion
9 oz/250 g whole grain spelt pasta
1 tbsp olive oil
Generous ¾ cup/ 200 ml light/ single (soy) cream
Salt and freshly ground pepper

Indian **Lentil** and **Chard** Curry

Serves 2

1 bunch chard
1 onion
1 clove of garlic
1 tbsp olive oil
1 cup/7 oz/200 g
red lentils
1¼ cups/300 ml
coconut milk
1¼ cups/300 ml
vegetable broth
(stock)
1 tbsp lime juice

■ Wash and clean the chard and cut into strips. Peel the onion and dice finely. Peel and crush the garlic.

■ Heat the olive oil in a pan and gently fry the onion and garlic until translucent.

■ Add the red lentils and the chard, and deglaze with the coconut milk, vegetable broth, and lime juice. Bring back to a boil then simmer over low heat for 10 minutes, stirring occasionally, until the liquid has been absorbed.

■ Rinse the cilantro (coriander), pat dry, strip off the leaves, and chop finely.

■ Stir in and season with the spices, salt, and pepper, to taste. Fold in the cilantro, and transfer the curry to two plates.

½ bunch cilantro
(coriander)
Ground cumin
Chili powder
Curry powder
Salt and freshly
ground pepper

When chard is out of season you can replace it with leaf spinach, and parsley is fine to use as an alternative to cilantro.

Colorful **Quinoa** Salad

Serves 2

½ cup/100 g
white quinoa
Generous
¾ cup/200 ml
vegetable broth
(stock)
1 carrot
½ cucumber
1 yellow bell
pepper

■ Rinse the quinoa in a strainer under cold running water until the water runs clear. Cook the quinoa in the vegetable broth for 15 minutes.

■ Wash and trim the carrot, cucumber, bell pepper, radishes, and tomatoes. Peel the carrot, and seed the bell pepper. Cut the vegetables into bite-size pieces. Peel the onion and cut into fine strips. Wash the parsley, pat dry, strip off the leaves, and chop finely.

■ Pass the cooked quinoa through a strainer. Mix the vegetables with the quinoa in a salad bowl. Mix the olive oil and lemon juice to make a dressing, season to taste with salt and pepper, and fold into the salad.

½ bunch
radishes
2 tomatoes
1 red onion
½ bunch parsley
3 tbsp olive oil
Juice of ½ lemon
Salt and freshly
ground pepper

This colorful quinoa salad makes a perfect summer dish and can be eaten either warm or cold.

It's a healthy treat for kids as well, and is vegan and gluten-free.

Naturally
fresh
simply
good

Special:
Pseudocereals

Pseudocereals contain no gluten (a sticky protein), making them suitable for people with allergies. In addition to vegetable protein, they also provide high-quality carbohydrates and dietary fiber, healthy essential fatty acids, B vitamins, and plenty of minerals such as iron, calcium, potassium, and magnesium. The best-known pseudocereals are quinoa, amaranth, and buckwheat.

Quinoa has a whole range of uses. It is cooked like rice and can be eaten as a side dish or in porridge, a burger, casserole, or salad. It's important to wash quinoa thoroughly before cooking to rinse out all the bitter compounds (saponins) it contains. These substances can cause food intolerances in toddlers under two years of age in particular, so they should not eat quinoa. It is available in white, red, and black, and has a nutty flavor.

Amaranth can be eaten cooked or puffed. Puffed amaranth is tasty in muesli or Overnight Oats and is easy to make: place the grains in a saucepan with no oil or fat and heat until they stop puffing. Cooked amaranth can be served as a side dish or porridge and is delicious in salads.

Buckwheat has a slightly nutty flavor and can be either sweet or savory. Roast it to add to muesli, yogurt, quark, or mascarpone cheese, or use it cooked in soups, or baked for pancakes or in burgers.

Celery Root **Schnitzel** in **Coconut Batter** with **Curry** and **Mango** Sauce

Serves 2

1 celery root
[celeriac]
1²⁄₃ cups/400 ml
coconut milk
Generous
¾ cup/200 ml
vegetable broth
[stock]
1 cup/200 g
whole grain rice
1 mango
1 tbsp curry
powder
Salt and freshly
ground pepper
½ cup/50 g
coconut flour
2 tbsp coconut
oil

■ Bring a pan of water to a boil. Peel and wash the celery root [celeriac] and cut into slices ⅝–¾ inch/1.5–2 cm thick. Add the slices to the boiling water and simmer over medium heat for 10 minutes.

■ Meanwhile, bring 1¼ cups/300 ml coconut milk and 7 tbsp/ 100 ml vegetable broth to a boil in a second pan. Add the rice and simmer over medium heat for 15 minutes.

■ Trim the mango flesh from the seed and peel off the skin. Whiz the flesh with 7 tbsp/100 ml coconut milk and 7 tbsp/100 ml veg- etable broth in a blender or food processor, then transfer to a small pan and bring back to a boil. Stir in the curry powder and season to taste with salt and pepper.

■ Drain the celery root slices through a colander, refresh in cold water, and pat dry. Stir the coconut flour into generous ¾ cup/200 ml water and press the coating onto the celery root slices with your hands.

■ Heat the coconut oil in a skillet and fry the celery root schnit- zels on both sides for 2–3 minutes, until golden brown. Serve with the rice and the mango curry sauce.

These schnitzels also taste really good with kohlrabi instead of celery root. The dish is lactose-free, gluten-free, and vegan. The coconut flour used to make the batter is naturally gluten-free and particularly nutritious; it is extremely good for boiling or baking.

Asian-Style **Mushrooms** and **Vegetables** in **Coconut Sauce**

Serves 2

1 oz/25 g
dried oyster
mushrooms
1 oz/25 g
dried shiitake
mushrooms
6 scallions
(spring onions)
1 clove of garlic
2 carrots
¼ Chinese
cabbage
1 red bell pepper
1 tsp coconut oil
1 cup/100 g peas
(frozen)

■ Rinse the dried mushrooms under cold running water and soak in water for about 20 minutes. Drain well in a strainer.

■ Meanwhile, wash and trim the scallions and cut into rings. Peel and crush the clove of garlic. Wash, peel, and trim the carrots, then cut into thin slices.

■ Strip the Chinese cabbage leaves from the stalk, cut into strips, wash, and drain. Trim, seed, and wash the bell pepper and cut into strips.

■ Heat the coconut oil in a skillet. Briefly fry the scallions and the garlic before adding the prepared vegetables, the peas, and the mushrooms. Fry for 5 minutes, stirring occasionally.

■ Add the coconut milk and soy sauce and simmer for another 10 minutes. Transfer the vegetables to two plates and garnish with sesame seeds.

1²⁄₃ cups/400 ml
coconut milk
2 tbsp soy sauce
1 tbsp sesame
seeds, to garnish

Italian **Pasta Salad**

Serves 2

1¼ cups/125 g whole wheat farfalle
3½ oz/100 g arugula (rocket)
1 red onion
3½ oz/100 g cherry tomatoes
3½ oz/100 g sundried tomatoes

■ Cook the whole wheat farfalle in plenty of water, according to the directions on the package and until al dente. Meanwhile, wash the arugula, pat dry, sort, and trim off the stalks. Peel the onion and cut into thin strips. Wash the cherry tomatoes and cut in half. Cut the sundried tomatoes into pieces. Halve the olives.

■ Drain the pasta through a colander and refresh in cold water. Mix with the prepared ingredients in a salad bowl. Coarsely shred the Parmesan. Stir the olive oil and Parmesan into the salad and season to taste with salt and pepper.

½ cup/100 g pitted black olives
2 oz/50 g Parmesan
2 tbsp olive oil
Salt and freshly ground pepper

Savoy Cabbage Wraps with Carrots and Avocado Dip

Serves 2

4 Savoy cabbage
leaves
14 oz/400 g
carrots
2 shallots
2 tbsp olive oil
⅓ cup/30 g
slivered almonds
2 avocados
2 cloves of garlic
Juice of ½ lemon
Salt and freshly
ground pepper

■ Bring plenty of water to a boil in a pan. Wash the Savoy cabbage leaves, immerse in the boiling water for 2 minutes, drain through a colander, and refresh in cold water. Drain the leaves and pat dry with a cloth.

■ Wash, peel, and trim the carrots, then cut into thin slices with a vegetable peeler. Peel the shallots and dice finely. Heat the olive oil in a skillet and fry the shallots and the almonds for 2–3 minutes. Add the carrot slices and 2 tbsp water, and simmer over medium heat for 5 minutes, stirring occasionally.

■ Meanwhile, halve the avocados, remove the pit and the skin, cut the flesh into large pieces and spoon into a bowl. Peel and crush the garlic and add to the avocado, along with the lemon juice. Mix everything with a fork, crushing the avocado. Season the avocado dip with salt and pepper, to taste.

■ Arrange the Savoy cabbage leaves on plates and coat with the avocado dip. Place the carrot mixture on top and serve. The Savoy Cabbage Wraps can also be folded up and and eaten with the fingers.

Ratatouille with Kidney Beans

Serves 2

2 cups/400 g dried kidney beans
½ eggplant (aubergine)
1 zucchini (courgette)
14 oz/400 g tomatoes
1 red bell pepper
1 carrot
1 onion
4 tbsp olive oil
Generous ¾ cup/200 ml vegetable broth (stock)
1 clove of garlic
1 bunch herbes de Provence
1¾ oz/50 g sundried tomatoes
Salt and freshly ground pepper

■ Soak the dried kidney beans in plenty of water for 12 hours in advance of cooking the dish. Drain and bring fresh water to a boil in a saucepan. Boil the beans vigorously for 10 minutes then reduce the heat and simmer over medium heat for 45 minutes, or until tender. Drain well.

■ Meanwhile, trim and wash the eggplant, zucchini, tomatoes, bell pepper, and carrot. Peel the carrot, remove the seeds from the bell pepper. Cut the vegetables and tomatoes into bite-size cubes. Peel the onion and dice finely.

■ Heat the olive oil in a pan and fry the onion until translucent. Add the vegetables and tomatoes and cook for 2–3 minutes, then deglaze the pan with the vegetable broth and simmer over medium heat for another 15 minutes.

■ Peel and crush the garlic, wash the herbs, pat dry, strip off the leaves, and chop finely. Cut the sundried tomatoes into thin strips. Finally, add the kidney beans, sundried tomato strips, garlic, and herbs, warm through briefly, and season to taste with salt and pepper.

Ratatouille is a classic vegan dish from southern France to which I have added a twist with the addition of beans, making it a filling main meal. The fresh herbs lend it extra zing. Herbes de Provence as a dried bouquet can be purchased at markets or in well-stocked organic grocery stores. The mix varies, but typically includes basil, marjoram, oregano, rosemary, lavender, sage, thyme, bay leaf, and savory.

Fried **Green Beans**
and **Chanterelles**

Serves 2

3 tbsp/25 g
pine nuts
1 onion
7 oz/200 g green
beans
1 tbsp olive oil
½ cup/60 g
buckwheat
2 cups/500 ml
vegetable broth
(stock)
3½ oz/100 g
chanterelles
½ bunch thyme
Salt and freshly
ground pepper

■ Dry-fry the pine nuts in a skillet and put to one side. Peel the onion and dice finely. Wash and trim the green beans and cut into pieces.

■ Heat the olive oil in a skillet and gently fry the onion until translucent. Add the buckwheat, deglaze with the vegetable broth, and add the beans. Simmer the dish for 20 minutes, stirring occasionally.

■ Meanwhile, wash and trim the chanterelles. Wash the thyme and pat dry before stripping off the leaves. Add the mushrooms to the saucepan after 20 minutes and simmer everything for another 10 minutes, stirring continuously. Stir in the thyme leaves and season to taste with salt and pepper. Serve sprinkled with the pine nuts.

Garbanzo Bean Salad with Tomatoes

Serves 2

⅔ cup/140 g
dried garbanzo
beans
(chickpeas)
14 oz/400 g
red and yellow
cherry tomatoes
½ lemon
4 tbsp olive oil
Salt and freshly
ground pepper
½ bunch basil
½ bunch parsley

■ Soak the garbanzo beans in water for 24 hours, then drain through a strainer and rinse. Place in a saucepan of fresh water and cook for 30–40 minutes, or until tender.

■ Meanwhile, wash the cherry tomatoes and cut in half. Squeeze the lemon. To make the dressing, mix the lemon juice and olive oil, and season to taste with salt and pepper. Wash the basil and parsley, pat dry, strip off the leaves, and chop finely.

■ Once the garbanzo beans are cooked, drain them through a colander, rinse in cold water, and drain well. Mix with the cherry tomatoes in a salad bowl. Fold in the dressing and serve sprinkled with the chopped basil and parsley leaves.

This salad is healthy as well as being extremely easy to transport and eat on the go. If you are pushed for time, use 2 cups/350 g cooked garbanzo beans from a jar.

Spinach and **Quinoa Burger** with **Avocado Dip**

Makes 4

For the burgers
4 burger buns
(page 114)
½ cup/100 g
quinoa
1 cup/250 ml
vegetable broth
(stock)
7 oz/200 g
spinach (frozen)
1 onion
1 clove of garlic
1 tbsp mustard
2 tbsp whole
grain spelt flour
6–8 tbsp whole
grain oat flakes
½ bunch parsley
Freshly grated
nutmeg
Salt and freshly
ground pepper
2 tbsp sunflower
oil
Tomato ketchup

**For the
avocado dip**
1 avocado
2 tbsp lemon
juice
Salt and freshly
ground pepper

For the garnish
1 tomato
¼ cucumber
Cress
2 handfuls mixed
salad leaves

■ Place the quinoa in a strainer and rinse under cold running water until the water runs clear. Cook the quinoa for 15 minutes in the vegetable broth. Defrost the spinach (use the microwave for speed) and squeeze the liquid out through a strainer. Peel the onion and garlic and cut into fine dice.

■ Place the spinach in a food processor along with the onion, garlic, mustard, and spelt flour and process to a smooth texture. Transfer the mixture to a bowl. Stir in the cooked quinoa and the oat flakes to make a firm patty. Depending on the amount of liquid, you may need to add a greater or lesser quantity of oat flakes. Wash the parsley, pat dry, strip off the leaves, and chop finely. Mix the parsley into the burger mixture and season to taste with nutmeg, salt, and pepper.

■ Shape the mixture into 4 burgers and fry on both sides in hot sunflower oil in a skillet.

■ For the avocado dip, cut the avocado in half, remove the pit, and spoon out the flesh. Using a hand blender, whiz the avocado, lemon juice, and salt and pepper to taste to a smooth puree.

■ To make the salad garnish, wash the tomato and the cucumber, cut out the base of the stalk from the tomato, and cut the tomato and cucumber into slices. Snip off some cress from its bed, wash along with the salad and pat dry, tearing the salad leaves into bite-size strips if necessary.

■ Cut the burger buns in half. Spread the bases with tomato ketchup (see page 114). Place the spinach and quinoa burger on top of the bases and garnish with salad, slices of tomato and cucumber, and cress. Spread the top halves of the buns with the avocado dip and place on top of the burgers.

Burger **Buns**

Makes 4

Generous ¾ cup/
125 g whole grain
spelt flour
Generous ¾ cup/
125 g whole
grain Khorasan
(kamut) flour
2 tsp/⅓ oz/10 g
fresh yeast
1 tsp honey
½ tsp salt
2 tbsp sunflower
oil

■ Sift the spelt and Khorasan flours into a mixer bowl and make a well in the center. Crumble the yeast, stir into 3½ tbsp/50 ml lukewarm water along with the honey, and pour into the well. Mix with a little flour and let the yeast mixture stand at room temperature for 10 minutes until it starts to foam.

■ Stir the salt into another 3½ tbsp/50 ml water and add to the bowl. Using the dough hook of your electric mixer, knead the dough for 5 minutes, then add the sunflower oil and knead for another 2 minutes. Knead the dough once more with your hands and shape into a ball. Cover the dough and let rise for 2 hours at room temperature, until it has doubled in volume.

■ Divide the dough into 4 pieces and shape into buns. Line a baking sheet with parchment paper and spray with water. Place the burger buns on top, cover, and let prove for another hour at room temperature. Preheat the oven to 347°F/175°C then bake the burger buns for 20 minutes. Remove from the oven and let cool on a wire rack.

■ Cut the buns in half and fill with the spinach and quinoa burgers, ketchup, avocado dip, and salad (page 112).

Tomato **Ketchup**

**Makes approx.
1 cup/250 ml**

11 oz/300 g
tomatoes
1 red onion
1 dried chili
1 tbsp olive oil
2 tbsp agave
syrup
1 tbsp tomato
paste
1 tsp sweet
paprika
Salt and freshly
ground pepper

■ Wash the tomatoes, cut out the base of the stalks, and dice the tomatoes. Peel the onion and dice finely. Crumble the dried chili finely.

■ Heat the olive oil in a pan, add the onion, and fry gently until translucent. Add the agave syrup and caramelize the onions. Add the tomatoes, tomato paste, and chili, and bring to a boil.

■ Simmer over low heat for 20 minutes, stirring occasionally. Liquidize with a stick blender until smooth and season with the paprika, and salt and pepper to taste.

Red Beet **Tartare**

Serves 2

1 large red
beet (approx.
9 oz/250 g; or
1 precooked and
vacuum-packed
red beet)
1 shallot
½ bunch thyme
⅔ cup/150 g
ricotta
1 tsp honey
1 tbsp olive oil
Salt and freshly
ground pepper

■ Bring a pan of water to a boil and simmer the red beet over medium heat for about 45 minutes. Meanwhile, peel the shallot and dice finely. Wash and pat dry the thyme, then strip off the leaves.

■ Place the ricotta in a bowl, stir in the honey, olive oil, and thyme leaves, and season to taste with salt and pepper. When the beet is cooked, drain through a colander, and refresh in cold water.

■ Trim off a small section at the top and bottom of the beet and remove the skin with your fingers. It's best to wear disposable gloves for this as it will leave stubborn stains. Dice the beet finely and fold into the ricotta mixture—make sure to mix everything well.

■ Place a metal ring (3¼ inches/8 cm) on a serving plate, Place half the beet tartare inside and press down with a fork, repeating the process on a second plate. Remove the rings before serving. This will go well with a leaf salad.

Potatoes and Zucchini in a **Creamy** Sauce

Serves 2

11/4 lb/600 g
potatoes
1 lb/500 g
zucchini
(courgettes)
2 tbsp mustard
seeds
½ bunch dill
2 tbsp butter
2 tbsp whole
grain rye flour
4½ oz/125 g
mustard
¼ cup/50 g
cream cheese
Salt and freshly
ground pepper

■ Peel, wash, and dice the potatoes. Bring 1⅔ cups/400 ml water to a boil in a saucepan and cook the potatoes for 10 minutes until done. Wash and trim the zucchini, dice, and add to the water along with the mustard seeds. Simmer everything for another 10 minutes, stirring occasionally.

■ Meanwhile, wash the dill, pat dry, strip off the leaves, and chop. Melt the butter in a pan. Whisk in the flour with a hand whisk over low heat. Stir in the mustard and the cream cheese, to make a creamy sauce. Add the chopped dill leaves and season to taste with salt and pepper.

■ Drain the vegetables through a colander and transfer to a serving dish. Fold in the sauce and serve immediately.

For a vegan version, make the dish according to the recipe but with vegan margarine instead of butter and vegetable cream instead of cream cheese.

White Bean Soup
with Whole Wheat Pasta

Serves 2

½ cup/100 g
dried white
beans
2 cups/500 ml
vegetable broth
(stock)
1 onion
1 carrot
Approx. 7 oz/
200 g celery root
(celeriac)

■ Soak the white beans in water overnight. The next day, drain the beans through a strainer, transfer to a pan with the vegetable broth, bring to a boil, and simmer over low heat for 1 hour.

■ Peel and dice the onion. Trim, peel, wash, and dice the carrot and celery root. Add the onion, celery root, and carrot to the beans after they have been cooking for 40 minutes and simmer. After 50 minutes' cooking time, add the macaroni to the pan and cook in the broth, adding a little water if necessary.

■ Wash the parsley, pat dry, strip off the leaves, chop finely, and add to the pan. Stir the olive oil into the soup and season to taste with salt and pepper.

1 cup/100 g
whole wheat
macaroni
2 sprigs parsley
2 tbsp olive oil
Salt and freshly
ground pepper

Stuffed **Rondini** with **Tomato Rice**

Serves 2

2 rondini (round zucchini/ courgettes)
1 onion
1 clove of garlic
2 carrots
1 tbsp olive oil
½ cup/100 g whole grain rice
2 tomatoes
2 tbsp tomato paste
3½ oz/100 g feta
½ bunch parsley
1 tsp dried oregano
1 tsp sweet paprika
Salt and freshly ground pepper

■ Wash the rondini, cut out a "lid" from the top, and spoon out the flesh. Peel the onion and garlic, chop the onion finely, and crush the garlic. Trim, peel, and wash the carrots and slice finely.

■ Heat the olive oil in a pan and fry the onion and garlic for 1 minute. Add the rice and deglaze the pan with 1⅔ cups/400 ml water. Add the carrots to the pan and simmer everything for 15 minutes, stirring occasionally.

■ Meanwhile, wash and trim the tomatoes, cut into bite-size pieces, and add to the pan with the tomato paste. Simmer for another 5 minutes, stirring continuously. The water should have evaporated by the time the tomatoes are cooked.

■ Preheat the oven to 390°F/200°C or 355°F/180°C fan. Cut the feta into cubes. Wash the parsley, pat dry, strip off the leaves, and chop finely. Remove the saucepan with the rice from the heat, fold in the feta, parsley, oregano, and sweet paprika, and season to taste with salt and pepper. Stuff the rondini with the rice mixture and cook in the preheated oven for 20 minutes, or until tender.

Just like zucchini, rondini are part of the pumpkin and squash family. They also look a lot like their cousins and are often called "round zucchini." The biggest difference between the two is that, unlike zucchini, rondini cannot be eaten raw.

Zucchini **Pilaf** with **Cranberries**

Serves 2

6 tbsp/50 g pine nuts
14 oz/400 g zucchini (courgettes)
2 tbsp olive oil
1 onion
⅓ cup/50 g dried cranberries
½ cup/100 g whole grain rice
1⅔ cups/400 ml vegetable broth (stock)
½ bunch parsley
1 cup/100 g peas (frozen)
1 pinch ground turmeric
1 tsp curry powder
1 tsp whole cumin seeds
Salt and freshly ground pepper

■ Briefly dry-fry the pine nuts in a nonstick skillet, remove, and set aside. Wash and trim the zucchini, and cut into slices ¾ inch/2 cm thick. Heat 1 tbsp olive oil in the skillet and fry the zucchini slices on both sides until golden. Remove, cover, and set aside.

■ Peel the onion and dice finely. Heat the remaining olive oil in the skillet and gently fry the onion. Add the cranberries and the rice, add the vegetable broth and use it to deglaze the pan. Cover and simmer over low heat for about 15 minutes.

■ Meanwhile, wash the parsley, strip off the leaves, pat dry, and chop finely. Stir the zucchini slices and the peas into the rice and simmer for 2–3 minutes. Fold in the parsley and the spices, and season to taste with salt and pepper. Garnish the pilaf with the pine nuts and serve.

Moroccan
Spinach Salad

Serves 2

2 handfuls fresh
leaf spinach
1 red onion
1 pomegranate
3½ oz/100 g feta
½ bunch parsley
3 tbsp/20 g
walnut kernels
Salt and freshly
ground pepper
2 tbsp olive oil

■ Wash, drain, and sort the spinach, and arrange on a serving plate or in a salad bowl. Peel the onion and cut into strips.

■ Cut the pomegranate in half and place in a bowl filled with water. Using your fingers, separate out the seeds under the water; they will sink to the bottom while the dividing membranes float to the surface. Remove the membranes and drain the pomegranate seeds in a strainer.

■ Cut the feta into cubes. Wash the parsley, pat dry, strip off the leaves, and chop finely. Arrange the onion, pomegranate seeds, and feta on the spinach. Garnish with the walnuts and chopped parsley, season with salt and pepper, to taste, and drizzle with the olive oil.

Naturally
fresh
simply
good

Special:
Raw and **Tasty**

Boring carrot sticks and so-called rabbit food are yesterday's news. The raw food movement has developed into a delicious and varied gourmet cooking style over the last few years. Along with salads, you can now enjoy raw food soups, wraps, pizza, and ice creams rather than having to deny yourself.

There are plenty of theories about what a raw food diet is exactly, but it is generally agreed that foods that have been processed or heated above 108°F/42°C are not part of it. Gentle preparation means that all the nutrients are preserved and heat-sensitive elements such as secondary plant substances are retained, unaltered.

Many studies have shown that a high proportion of raw food in the diet is good for the body, and fresh fruit and vegetables should make up the majority of a healthy diet. Raw food will ensure you have clearer skin, feel better, and enjoy greater vitality and well-being.

In addition to fruit, vegetables, [wild] herbs, shoots, and cold-pressed oils, you will also find nuts, dried fruit, seeds, and kernels also qualify as raw food. Depending on what you consider raw, even milk, fish, and meat can be included, for example in the form of unpasteurized milk [products], carpaccio, or tartare. Most raw food fans follow a vegetarian or vegan diet, however.

Chard Speltotto

Serves 2

2 shallots
4 tbsp olive oil
1 quart/1 l
vegetable broth
(stock)
1½ cups/150 g
spelt grains
1 bunch chard
½ tsp freshly
grated nutmeg
Salt and freshly
ground pepper
2 tbsp freshly
shredded
Parmesan

■ Peel the shallots and dice finely. Heat 2 tbsp olive oil in a large pan and gently fry the shallots for 2–3 minutes, then deglaze the pan with the vegetable broth. Add the spelt grains and simmer in the vegetable broth for 20 minutes, stirring continuously.

■ Meanwhile, wash the chard, trim off the stalk ends, and cut the rest into strips. Add the chard to the spelt and simmer everything for another 10 minutes, until the spelt grains are creamy but still al dente. Add the nutmeg, season to taste with salt and pepper, and stir in the remaining olive oil and the Parmesan.

For the vegan version, make the speltotto in the same way but leave out the Parmesan; instead, finely chop pine nuts or almonds, nutritional yeast flakes, bread crumbs, and 1 pinch salt in a food processor and fold in to finish off the dish.

Vegan version

2 shallots
4 tbsp olive oil
1 quart/1 l
vegetable broth
(stock)
1½ cups/150 g
spelt grains
1 bunch chard
½ tsp freshly
grated nutmeg
Salt and freshly
ground pepper
¾ cup/100 g pine
nuts or peeled
almonds
Scant ½ cup/25 g
nutritional yeast
flakes
¼ cup/15 g bread
crumbs

Corn Soup

Serves 2

1 corn cob (or
7 oz/200 g
canned corn)
2 small
potatoes
(approx. 7 oz/
200 g)
1 onion
1 tbsp olive oil
2 cups/500 ml
vegetable broth
(stock)
1 yellow bell
pepper
½ bunch chives
½ cup/125 ml
soy/oat cream
Salt and freshly
ground pepper
Freshly grated
nutmeg

■ Remove the leaves and fibers from the corn cob and cook the corn in boiling water for 5 minutes. Trim off the corn kernels with a sharp knife.

■ Peel the potatoes and cut into pieces. Peel the onion and dice finely. Heat the olive oil in a pan and gently fry the onion. Add the potatoes, deglaze with vegetable broth, and simmer over medium heat for 10 minutes.

■ Trim, seed, and wash the bell pepper, and cut into pieces. Add the bell pepper and corn kernels to the soup and simmer every-thing for another 5 minutes. Wash the chives, pat dry, and cut into very small rings.

■ Add the soy/oat cream to the soup, liquidize everything, and season to taste with salt, pepper, and nutmeg. Stir in half the chives and serve the soup garnished with the remaining chives.

Forest Mushrooms on Potato and Jerusalem Artichoke Puree

Serves 2

Generous
1 lb/500 g mixed
mushrooms (e.g.
white or brown,
chanterelles,
oyster)
1 onion
½ bunch chives
9 oz/250 g
Jerusalem
artichokes
9 oz/250 g
potatoes
2 tbsp olive oil
Salt and freshly
ground pepper
1 pinch freshly
grated nutmeg

■ Clean and trim the mushrooms, cutting any large ones into bite-size pieces. Peel the onion and dice finely. Wash the chives, pat dry, and chop finely.

■ Peel and wash the Jerusalem artichokes and potatoes, dice coarsely, and cook in boiling water for 15 minutes.

■ Meanwhile, heat 1 tbsp olive oil in a skillet and gently fry the onion until translucent before adding the mushrooms. Cook for about 10 minutes, stirring occasionally, then stir in the chives and season to taste with salt and pepper.

■ Drain the Jerusalem artichokes and potatoes through a colander and return them to the pan. Add 1 tbsp olive oil, and mash with a potato masher. Add the nutmeg and season to taste with salt. Transfer the potato and Jerusalem artichoke puree to two plates and arrange the mushrooms on top.

Jerusalem artichoke is a root vegetable that looks like ginger root but is botanically related to the sunflower. Jerusalem artichokes are native to North and Central America and are thought to have reached Europe at the beginning of the 17th century. Here, they were an important basic foodstuff until supplanted by the potato. Jerusalem artichokes are slowly regaining their place in weekly markets and well-stocked organic grocery stores and supermarkets. They have a slightly sweet and nutty flavor and are very filling, thanks to their high content of dietary fiber. They can be eaten raw and unpeeled, or boiled, fried, and roasted. They can be kept in the refrigerator for only a few days.

Pumpkin **Quinotto** with Sage **Sauce**

Serves 2

1 cup/7 oz/200 g white or red quinoa
½ red kuri squash
1 red onion
1 tbsp olive oil
2 cups/500 ml vegetable broth [stock]
⅔ cup/150 g cream cheese
10 sage leaves
3 tbsp cornstarch [cornflour]

2 tbsp freshly shredded Parmesan
Freshly ground pepper
Freshly grated nutmeg
2 tbsp pumpkin seeds

■ Place the quinoa in a strainer and rinse under cold running water until the water runs clear; this will remove its bitter compounds. Wash, seed, and dice the red kuri squash. Peel the onion and chop finely.

■ Heat the olive oil in a pan, gently fry the onion, and add the cubes of squash. Fry for 2–3 minutes then deglaze the pan with 1⅔ cups/400 ml vegetable broth and add the rinsed quinoa. Cook for 15 minutes until tender, stirring occasionally.

■ Meanwhile, to make the sage sauce, bring the remaining vegetable broth to a boil in a small pan. Stir in the cream cheese. Wash the sage leaves, pat dry, chop finely, and stir in. Stir the cornstarch into a little cold water and use it to thicken the sauce.

■ Stir the Parmesan into the quinotto and season with pepper and nutmeg to taste. Dress the quinotto with the sage sauce and sprinkle with pumpkin seeds.

Colorful **Quinoa Tabbouleh** with **Pomegranate**

Serves 2

½ cup/100 g
red quinoa
Generous ¾ cup/
200 ml vegetable
broth (stock)
1 tomato
½ cucumber
1 avocado
2 tbsp lemon
juice
½ pomegranate
1 small red onion
1–2 sprigs mint
2–3 sprigs
parsley
4 tbsp sliced
almonds
2 tbsp olive oil
1 tsp lemon juice
1 tsp runny
honey
Freshly ground
pepper

■ Place the quinoa in a strainer and rinse under cold running water until the water runs clear. This will remove its bitter compounds. Heat the vegetable broth in a pan and cook the quinoa for 15 minutes until done.

■ Meanwhile, wash and dice the tomato and cucumber. Cut the avocado in half, remove the pit and the skin, and dice the flesh. Drizzle the avocado with the 2 tbsp lemon juice.

■ Place the pomegranate half in a bowl filled with water. Using your fingers, separate out the seeds under the water; they will sink to the bottom while the dividing membranes float to the surface. Strain the pomegranate seeds, remove the membranes and discard.

■ Peel the onion and cut into rings. Wash the mint and parsley, pat dry, strip off the leaves, and chop finely.

■ Drain the cooked quinoa well through a strainer. Mix with the other prepared ingredients in a bowl. Briefly dry-fry the sliced almonds in a skillet.

■ To make the dressing, stir the olive oil into the 1 tsp lemon juice and the honey, and pour over the tabbouleh. Season with pepper to taste and serve sprinkled with the sliced almonds.

As a variation, you could add fresh sprouts instead of the parsley.

Fall Salad

Serves 2

2 tsp honey
2 slices goat
cheese (1¾ oz/
50 g)
1 sprig fresh
rosemary
2 figs
3 tbsp/25 g pine
nuts
5½ oz/150 g
lamb's lettuce
(mache)
2 tbsp olive oil
1 tbsp fig or
wholegrain
mustard
Salt and freshly
ground pepper

■ Preheat the oven to 355°F/180°C or 320°F/160°C fan. Drizzle 1 tsp honey over each of the slices of goat cheese. Cut the rosemary sprig in half and place on top.

■ Wash and dry the figs and make a cross-shaped cut at the base of the stalk. Place the figs and slices of goat cheese on a baking sheet lined with parchment paper and warm in the oven for 15 minutes.

■ Briefly dry-fry the pine nuts in a skillet and set aside. Dry the lamb's lettuce in a salad spinner and sort.

■ To make the dressing, mix the olive oil, fig or wholegrain mustard, and 1 tsp honey in a bowl and season to taste with salt and pepper.

■ Arrange the lamb's lettuce in a salad bowl or on a serving plate. Pour the dressing on top and mix in. Place the goat cheese and the figs on the lamb's lettuce and sprinkle with the pine nuts.

Tip

Use dried figs when fresh figs are out of season. The salad is also very tasty with arugula (rocket) instead of lamb's lettuce, and dried cranberries add extra zing. Fig mustard is an Italian delicacy and is available in many well-stocked delicatessens. If you cannot find it, use wholegrain mustard instead.

Frittata with **Green Asparagus**

Serves 2

1 shallot
1 tbsp olive oil
Generous 1 lb/
500 g green
asparagus
4 eggs
2 tbsp freshly
chopped
marjoram
3½ tbsp/50 ml
cream or soy
cream
Salt and freshly
ground pepper

■ Preheat the oven to 355°F/180°C or 320°F/160°C fan. Peel the shallot and chop finely. Heat the olive oil in a skillet and gently fry the shallot over medium heat for 1 minute until translucent, then set aside.

■ Trim off the woody ends of the asparagus and peel the bottom third of the spears. Cut the spears in half. Blanch in boiling water for 3 minutes until al dente. Drain well through a strainer and refresh in cold water. Arrange the asparagus spears in a round baking pan lined with parchment paper.

■ Whisk the eggs with the marjoram and the cream, and season with the salt, pepper, and nutmeg, to taste. Fold in the diced shallot. Pour all the ingredients over the asparagus and sprinkle with the Parmesan. Bake in the preheated oven for 30 minutes until golden brown. Take out the frittata, cut into slices and serve.

Freshly grated
nutmeg
3½ tbsp/1 oz/
25 g freshly
shaved
Parmesan

Red Beet with Lentil Stuffing

Serves 2

6 small red beets
1 shallot
½ carrot
½ parsnip
3½ oz/100 g
waxy potatoes
2½ tbsp olive oil
1 tsp curry
powder
Approx. 7 tbsp/
100 ml vegetable
broth (stock)
5½ cups/100 g
lentil sprouts
Salt and freshly
ground pepper

■ Peel the red beets and hollow out from the root end, leaving walls approx. ¼ inch/5 mm thick. It's best to wear gloves for this, as beet leaves stubborn stains. Simmer in water for 20 minutes until tender. Drain and set aside.

■ Meanwhile, peel and finely dice the shallot, carrot, parsnip, and potatoes. Heat 2 tbsp of the olive oil in a skillet and fry the shallot, carrot, and parsnip for 2 minutes. Mix in the potatoes and the curry powder and deglaze the pan with the vegetable broth. Simmer the mixture over medium heat for 15 minutes. Rinse the lentil sprouts, drain, add to the curry, and season with salt and pepper, to taste. Keep warm.

■ To make the sauce, peel and quarter the apple, discard the core, and dice the quarters finely. Chop the peanuts and fry with the apple in the remaining oil. Pour in the coconut milk and bring to a boil, then season to taste with salt and pepper. Stuff the drained beets with the vegetables and arrange on plates or dishes. Pour over the sauce and serve.

1 apple
Scant ¼ cup/25 g
unsalted peanuts
7 tbsp/100 ml
coconut milk

Baked **Yams** with Creamy **Avocado** and **Basil Filling**

Serves 2

2 yams
2 avocados
½ cup/100 g
cream cheese
6 sprigs basil
Salt and freshly
ground pepper
1 pomegranate

■ Preheat the oven to 390°F/200°C or 355°F/180°C fan. Wash the yams (but don't peel them). Using a fork, pierce several holes in the yams, place on a baking sheet lined with parchment paper, and bake for 45 minutes.

■ Meanwhile, cut the avocados in half, remove the pits, and spoon out the flesh. Crush the flesh lightly in a mixing bowl with a fork, add the cream cheese, and mix together.

■ Wash the basil, pat dry, and strip off the leaves. Reserve 2 leaves as a garnish and put the rest in the bowl. Liquidize with a hand blender, then season with salt and pepper, to taste, and fold into the cream cheese mixture.

■ Cut the pomegranate in half and place both halves in a bowl filled with water. Using your fingers, separate out the seeds under the water; they will sink to the bottom while the dividing membranes float to the surface. Remove the membranes and strain the pomegranate seeds.

■ Remove the cooked yams from the oven and pierce with a fork to check that they are cooked through. Cut them open lengthwise, transfer to two plates, and spoon in the creamy avocado and basil mixture; garnish with the pomegranate seeds and the basil leaves.

Sweet Chestnut and Potato Soup

Serves 2

14 oz/400 g
potatoes
7 oz/200 g
sweet chestnuts
(peeled and
precooked)
2 shallots
1 clove of garlic
1 tbsp butter
1 tbsp maple
syrup

■ Peel and dice the potatoes. Dice the sweet chestnuts. Peel the shallots and garlic and dice finely.

■ Heat the butter in a large pan and gently fry the shallots and garlic until translucent. Caramelize with the maple syrup, then add the potatoes and the sweet chestnuts and fry for 1 minute. Deglaze with the vegetable broth, bring to a boil, then simmer over medium heat for 15 minutes.

■ Stir in the cream cheese and liquidize with a hand blender. Add the cinnamon and season to taste with salt and pepper. Wash the parsley, pat dry, strip off the leaves, chop finely, and use to garnish the soup.

2 cups/500 ml
vegetable broth
(stock)
½ cup/100 g
cream cheese
1 pinch ground
cinnamon
Salt and freshly
ground pepper
2 sprigs parsley,
to garnish

Green Kale and Potato
Casserole

Serves 2

Generous
1 lb/500 g green
kale
Generous
1 lb/500 g
potatoes (two
thirds waxy, one
third mealy)
1 onion
2 tbsp olive oil
2 tbsp whole
grain rye or
spelt flour
⅔ cup/150 ml
vegetable broth
(stock)

■ Wash the kale, trim off the hard stalks and discard, and cut the leaves into bite-size pieces. Cook in boiling water for 10 minutes. Wash and peel the potatoes, then cut into thin slices with a grater or mandolin. Cook in boiling water for 10 minutes.

■ Meanwhile, preheat the oven to 390°F/200°C or 355°F/180°C fan. Peel the onion and dice finely. To make the mustard sauce, heat the olive oil in a small pan and briefly fry the onion. Stir in the flour and deglaze the pan with the vegetable broth. Add the mustard and simmer for 2–3 minutes, until thickened. Stir in the mustard seeds and nutmeg and season to taste with salt and pepper.

■ Strain the green kale and potatoes through a colander and briefly cool. Grease two small or one large Dutch oven or casserole and layer the potatoes and green kale in them. Pour over the mustard sauce and sprinkle with the cheese. Bake in the preheated oven for 20 minutes.

½ cup/125 ml
whole grain
mustard
1 tbsp mustard
seeds
1 pinch freshly
grated nutmeg
Salt and freshly
ground pepper
Butter or oil for
greasing
Scant 1 cup/
100 g freshly
shredded cheese
(e.g. Gouda,
Emmental, or
mozzarella)

Fig and Goat Cheese
Tarte Flambée

Serves 2

1²⁄₃ cups/9 oz/
250 g whole
grain spelt flour
2 tbsp olive oil
1 pinch salt
4 tbsp sour cream
2 figs
1 onion
3½ oz/100 g
goat cheese
(with rind)
2 sprigs thyme
4 walnut kernels
2 tbsp runny
honey

■ Preheat the oven to 390°F/200°C or 355°F/180°C fan. Sift the flour into a large bowl, then mix in the oil, salt, and ½ cup/125 ml lukewarm water and knead to form a dough. Divide in half and roll out thinly into circles. Line a baking sheet with parchment paper and place the circles of dough on top.

■ Top each tart with 2 tbsp sour cream. Wash and dry the figs and peel the onion. Cut the figs, onion, and goat cheese into thin slices and arrange on the circles of dough.

■ Wash the thyme, pat dry, and strip the leaves from the stalks. Chop the walnut kernels and scatter over the tarts. Drizzle everything with honey, and sprinkle over the thyme leaves. Bake the tarts in the preheated oven for 20 minutes.

Tartes flambées (or Flammkuchen, as they are known in German) are traditionally made with onions and bacon, but other interpretations taste just as good, whether savory, made with asparagus, squash, tomatoes, arugula, or olives, or sweet, made with apples or pears and cinnamon—there's no limit to topping choices.

Noodle Nests
with Walnut Sauce

Serves 2

2 shallots
1 clove of garlic
5½ oz/150 g leaf
spinach
1 bunch basil
1 cup/100 g
walnut kernels
1 tbsp olive oil,
plus extra, for
greasing
7 tbsp/100 ml
vegetable broth
(stock)
9 oz/250 g whole
wheat spaghetti
½ cup/100 g
(soy) yogurt
Salt and freshly
ground pepper
½ cup/50 g
freshly shredded
Gouda

■ Peel the shallots and garlic. Dice the shallots finely and crush the garlic. Sort the spinach and basil and wash. Cut the spinach into strips and tear the basil leaves. Reserve 2 or 3 walnut kernels for garnishing and grind the rest finely in a food processor.

■ Heat the olive oil in a skillet and fry the shallots, garlic, and ground walnuts for 1–2 minutes. Add the spinach and basil and fry over medium heat for 2–3 minutes, stirring occasionally. Deglaze with the vegetable broth and simmer for another 10 minutes.

■ Meanwhile, cook the spaghetti in plenty of boiling water according to the directions on the package, until al dente.

■ Preheat the oven to 390°F/200°C or 355°F/180°C fan. Grease 8 cups of a muffin pan. Drain the spaghetti through a colander. Squeeze out any excess water from the walnut and spinach mixture and stir in the (soy) yogurt. Season to taste with salt and pepper.

■ Twist the spaghetti to make small nests and place in the muffin pan. Place 1 tbsp of the walnut and spinach mixture on top and sprinkle with the cheese. Bake in the oven for 15 minutes. Remove the pan and arrange the noodle nests on plates. Decorate with the reserved walnuts.

chapter 5
Desserts and **Cakes**

The dessert is a much anticipated highlight after a tasty main course but can often contain any amount of sugar. Don't worry—you can still enjoy sweet treats by making homemade desserts and cakes healthier with a few simple tricks. In this chapter, I have suggested dessert recipes with clean ingredients like fruit, nuts, seeds, and milk (substitutes). Clean eating doesn't stop with baking, either—a dough made with whole grain Khorasan (kamut) flour or ground nuts instead of conventional wheat flour contains far more healthy nutrients—and tastes really good! My light desserts and cakes mean you will never have to have a guilty conscience: they fit right into the concept of clean eating. The Healthy Baking special on page 146 shows you some additional tips for simple ways to adapt your favorite cakes to the concept.

naturally
fresh
simply
good

Chocolate Bananas

Serves 2

7 oz/200 g
semisweet (plain)
chocolate (sugar-
free)
2 bananas
4 tbsp shredded
coconut
4 tbsp chopped
pistachios
4 tbsp dried
barberries (or
cranberries)

■ Fill a pan two-thirds full of water and heat to about 140° F/60° C. Chop the chocolate coarsely.

■ Place the chocolate in a metal or glass heatproof bowl and set the bowl over the pan of simmering water. Make sure the bottom of the bowl doesn't touch the water. Melt the chocolate, stirring with a spoon.

■ Peel the bananas and cut into thirds. Spread the shredded coconut, pistachios, and barberries out on separate plates. Dip the banana pieces first into the melted chocolate and then roll into the toppings (shredded coconut, chopped pistachios, or barberries) until coated.

■ Stick a toothpick into each chocolate-coated piece of banana and chill in the freezer for 30 minutes before serving.

Coconut **Raspberry** Dessert

Serves 2

1¼ cups/300 g
plain yogurt
1 cup/250 g
low-fat quark
or mascarpone
cheese
4 heaping tbsp
shredded
coconut

■ Mix half the yogurt and half the quark or mascarpone cheese in a bowl. Add the shredded coconut and 1 tsp raw cane sugar and mix together.

■ Using a stick blender, blend the remaining yogurt and quark or mascarpone, half the raspberries, and the remaining 1 tsp raw cane sugar in another bowl. Arrange alternating layers of coconut yogurt and raspberry yogurt in 2 glasses and decorate with the remaining raspberries.

2 tsp raw cane
sugar
2 cups/9 oz/
250 g raspberries

You can also use strawberries to make this dessert, and if berries are not in season, plums, mango, and pineapple would work very well, too. For a vegan version, use 2¼ cups/550 g soy yogurt instead of plain yogurt and quark or mascarpone cheese.

A Host of Healthy Pralines

For 6 piña colada pralines

⅔ cup/50 g shredded coconut
1¾ oz/50 g dried pineapple (with no added sugar)
⅓ cup/50 g unsalted cashews
5 dried dates
1 tbsp coconut oil

■ To make the piña colada, pistachio and barberry, and chocolate and vanilla pralines, place the ingredients in turn in a powerful food processor and whiz for a few seconds.

■ Clean the food processor thoroughly before adding the ingredients for the next praline. If you don't have a powerful food processor but only a hand blender or similar, soak the nuts for a few hours in advance.

■ Divide the piña colada and pistachio and barberry praline mixtures into 6 portions of each, and shape into balls.

■ Divide the chocolate and vanilla praline mixture into 4 portions, shape into balls, and roll the balls in cacao powder. Chill all the varieties of pralines in the refrigerator for 30 minutes before serving.

■ To make the large coconut and almond pralines, place the ingredients in a bowl and knead with your hands. Divide into 3 portions and shape into balls.

For 6 pistachio and barberry pralines

3 tbsp/20 g unsalted pistachios
¼ cup/20 g dried barberries
1¾ oz/50 g dried figs
3 tbsp/20 g walnut kernels
2 tbsp/20 g almond flour
Scant ¼ cup/ 20 g shredded coconut
1 tbsp coconut oil
Juice and shredded zest of ½ unwaxed lemon

These pralines—or "raw energy bites" or "energy balls"—are healthy, vegan, and delicious raw food options. They are also perfect to take as a gift if you are invited to someone's home. Raw cacao powder is considered one of the superfoods. The cocoa beans, which are ground to a powder, must not be heated above 108°F/42°C to preserve their precious vital ingredients. The cacao powder has a high concentration of antioxidants and contains the "happiness messengers" dopamine and serotonin.

For 4 chocolate and vanilla pralines

3½ oz/100 g dried dates (weighed with their pits)
2 tbsp raw cacao powder
½ tsp ground vanilla bean
1 tbsp raw cacao powder, for rolling

For 3 large coconut and almond pralines

⅓ cup/50 g almond flour
2 tbsp almond milk
⅔ cup/50 g shredded coconut
1 tbsp agave syrup
1 pinch vanilla powder

Naturally
fresh
simply
good

Special: Healthy **Baking**

Can you maintain a clean food diet and still enjoy all your favorite cakes? Yes, you can! You simply need to adapt your baking recipes to the concept of clean eating:

■ Apple sauce can be substituted for fat. In most recipes, you can substitute apple or other fruit purees for up to 30 percent of the fat.

■ Almost any cake can be baked with whole wheat flour instead of refined. This is especially easy with leavened doughs and sponge batters, although you will have to add a little more liquid: 10–20 percent water or milk (substitutes) will be enough as a rule. The dough should also rest for a while before being baked. Whole grain spelt and wheat flours are particularly suitable and can replace refined wheat flour on a 1:1 basis. As a cake made from whole grain flour looks darker, Khorasan (kamut) flour is a great alternative: the flour is light, even though it is made from the whole grain. Ground nuts can also stand in for some of the flour.

■ Reduce the quantity of sugar and go for raw cane sugar or coconut sugar instead of white sugar. Alternatively, you can also use honey: for ½ cup/100 g sugar you will need just 3½ tbsp/70 g honey.

■ Replace milk chocolate and white chocolate with semisweet (plain) chocolate with at least 70 percent cocoa content: it is healthy and fits in with the clean eating concept.

Spanish Almond Slice

**Makes 1 slice
(7 x 8¼ inches/
18 x 21 cm)**

2 cups/250 g
ground almonds
⅔ cup/50 g
chopped almonds
2 tbsp baking
powder
1 banana
3½ tbsp/50 g
butter or vegan
margarine
¼ cup/50 g raw
cane sugar
1 pinch vanilla
powder

■ Preheat the oven to 355°F/180°C or 320°F/160°C fan. Mix the ground and chopped almonds with the baking powder in a bowl.

■ In a second bowl, crush the banana with a fork, add the butter or margarine, raw cane sugar, and vanilla powder, and beat the mixture to a foam with a hand mixer. Stir in the almond milk then fold in the dry ingredients.

■ Grease a rectangular baking pan (7 x 8¼ inches/18 x 21 cm), fill with the batter, and smooth the top. Bake in the preheated oven for about 30 minutes until golden and firm. Remove and let cool in the pan on a wire rack.

Generous ¾ cup/
200 ml almond
milk
Fat for greasing

Tip

This cake is
gluten-free and,
if you use vege-
table margarine
instead of butter,
also vegan. If you
don't have a rect-
angular baking
pan, use a small
springform pan
(8 inches/20 cm).

Stuffed **Figs** with **Hazelnut** and **Chocolate Quark**

Serves 2

4 figs
Scant ½ cup/
100 g quark or
mascarpone
cheese
3 tbsp/20 g
hazelnuts
1 tsp cacao nibs

■ Carefully wash the figs and pat dry with a cloth. Cut off a "lid" from the stalk end of the figs and spoon out the flesh without damaging the skin.

■ Transfer the flesh to a bowl, crush with a fork, add this to the quark or mascarpone cheese, and mix. Chop the hazelnuts with a knife. Stir the nuts and the cacao nibs into the quark mixture.

■ Using a teaspoon, carefully stuff the figs with the hazelnut and chocolate quark stuffing. Decorate with the cacao nibs and serve.

Carrot Cake

Makes 1 cake (10½ inches/ 26 cm)

11 oz/300 g carrots
2 cups/300 g whole grain spelt flour
2 tbsp baking powder
7 tbsp/100 g peanut butter
⅓ cup/50 g unsalted peanuts
⅓ cup/50 g agave syrup
1 tsp ground cinnamon
1 pinch ground nutmeg
3 cardamom pods
Fat for greasing
Generous ¾ cup/ 200 g cream cheese
4 tbsp/60 g butter or vegan margarine
1 unwaxed orange

■ Preheat the oven to 355°F/180°C or 320°F/160°C fan. Peel the carrots and grate finely. Mix the carrots with the spelt flour, baking powder, and peanut butter in a bowl.

■ Chop the peanuts finely with a knife or whiz briefly in a food processor and add to the bowl. Then add the agave syrup, ½ tsp ground cinnamon, and the nutmeg.

■ Cut open the cardamom pods, remove the seeds, and grind with a mortar and pestle, then add to the mixture. Pour over ⅔ cup/150 ml water and mix everything together well using a hand mixer.

■ Grease a springform pan with butter or margarine. Pour in the batter and smooth the top. Bake on the middle shelf of the oven for 30 minutes.

■ Meanwhile, mix the cream cheese and the butter or margarine in a bowl. Zest the orange, squeeze out the juice, and add these to the mixture with the remaining ½ tsp ground cinnamon. Mix with a hand mixer and chill.

■ Remove the cake from the oven when ready and let cool in the mold on a wire rack for 30 minutes. Add the frosting to the cake and smooth down the top and sides with a knife. Chill the cake for 1 hour before serving.

This cake tastes even more delicious on the day after it is made—and it will keep for a few days in the refrigerator.

Chia Chocolate Pudding with Mint

Serves 2

4 sprigs mint
1²/₃ cups/400 ml almond milk
1 tsp raw cacao powder
1 tbsp agave syrup
4 tbsp chia seeds
2 tsp cacao nibs, to decorate

■ Wash the mint, pat dry, and strip off the leaves. Reserve a few leaves as a decoration, and chop the rest finely. Place these with the almond milk, cacao powder, and the agave syrup in a blender and whiz until smooth.

■ Stir in the chia seeds, transfer to 2 glasses or dishes, and chill in the refrigerator for at least 15 minutes to let the seeds swell up. The chia seeds will now form a gel, creating a thick pudding. To serve, decorate with the cacao nibs and mint.

Oatmeal Cookies

Makes 8–10 cookies

Scant 1¼ cups/ 100 g whole grain oat flakes (fine)
4½ tbsp/60 g raw cane sugar
¼ cup/60 g soy yogurt
Scant ⅓ cup/ 50 g whole grain rice flour

■ Preheat the oven to 347°F/175°C. Place all the ingredients in a bowl and, using your hands, work to a smooth dough.

■ Divide the dough into 8–10 portions and shape into balls. Press flat and arrange on a baking sheet lined with parchment paper.

■ Place the baking sheet in the oven and bake the cookies for 20 minutes. Let cool on the sheet.

If you have a powerful food processor, you can make whole grain rice flour very easily yourself. To do this, pour the whole grain rice into the food processor and whiz it to a fine flour. You will also find whole grain rice flour in well-stocked organic grocery stores, supermarkets, or alternatively, you can use cornmeal.

5 tbsp/80 g softened butter or vegan margarine
1 pinch vanilla powder
1 pinch salt

Fruit Salad with Red Quinoa and Vanilla Yogurt

Serves 2

Scant ½ cup/
80 g red quinoa
Generous ¾ cup/
200 g (soy)
yogurt
1 tsp raw cane
sugar
1 pinch vanilla
powder
14 oz/400 g
seasonal fruit
(e.g. banana,
Indian figs,
persimmon,
pomegranate,
grapes)
2 tbsp slivered
almonds

■ Place the quinoa in a strainer and rinse under cold running water until the water runs clear. Boil in generous ¾ cup/200 ml water for 15 minutes.

■ Meanwhile, mix the (soy) yogurt, raw cane sugar, and vanilla powder together. Wash the fruit, peeling and dicing if required.

■ Strain the cooked quinoa through a strainer and stir into the vanilla yogurt. Transfer the mixture to 2 bowls, pour the fruit salad on top, and sprinkle the slivered almonds over the dessert.

Red quinoa has a nutty and slighty sweet flavor that goes particularly well with both savory and sweet dishes. It works well as a main course or a dessert.

Spelt **Apple Cake** with **Almond Topping**

Makes 1 cake (10½ inches/ 26 cm)

For the batter
2 cups/300 g whole grain spelt flour
7 tbsp/100 g raw cane sugar
1 tsp baking powder
1 pinch salt
1 pinch vanilla powder
7 tbsp/100 g butter or vegan margarine
Scant ½ cup/ 100 g applesauce (with no added sugar)
Fat for greasing

■ To make the batter, sift the flour and mix with the raw cane sugar, baking powder, salt, and vanilla powder in a bowl. Cut the butter or margarine into pieces and add to the bowl. Add the applesauce and 3½ tbsp/50 ml water and mix to a batter with your hands (or a wooden spoon).

■ Preheat the oven to 355°F/180°C or 320°F/160°C fan. Grease a springform pan (10½ inches/26 cm) and spoon in the batter, smoothing the top and pulling it up slightly around the edge.

■ To make the filling, wash and core the apples, cut into cubes, and mix with the raw cane sugar and cinnamon. Arrange the apples evenly over the batter and bake the cake on the middle shelf of the oven for 45 minutes.

■ Meanwhile, make the almond topping: warm the cream, butter or margarine, and agave syrup in a small pan over medium heat (don't let it boil). Once the butter has melted, add the vanilla powder, cinnamon, and sliced almonds and stir until the almonds are coated in the mixture.

■ When the cake has been baking for 45 minutes, spread the almond topping evenly over the top of the apples and bake the cake for another 15 minutes. Remove the cake and let cool in the mold on a wire rack.

For the filling
1¾ lb/800 g apples
2 tbsp raw cane sugar
½ tsp ground cinnamon

For the almond topping
Generous ¾ cup/200 ml cream
2 tbsp/30 g butter or vegan margarine
1 tbsp agave syrup
1 pinch vanilla powder
1 pinch ground cinnamon
⅓ cup/200 g sliced almonds

If you like, you can add 7 tbsp/50 g raisins or ⅓ cup/50 g chopped nuts (e.g. hazelnuts or almonds) to the apple filling. You can also substitute 7 tbsp/100 g butter or margarine for the applesauce in the batter.

Lemon Muffins

Makes 12 muffins

Scant 2¼ cups/
330 g whole
grain Khorasan
(kamut) flour
4½ tbsp/60 g
raw cane sugar
1 tsp cornstarch
(cornflour)
1 tsp baking
powder
1 pinch salt
7 tbsp/100 g
butter or vegan
margarine
1 unwaxed lemon
Fat for greasing

■ Preheat the oven to 347°F/175°C or 311°F/155°C fan. Sift the flour and mix with the sugar, cornstarch, baking powder, and salt in a bowl. Cut the butter or margarine into pieces and add to the bowl.

■ Wash and dry the lemon. Grate the zest finely and then squeeze the juice. Add both to the batter, along with ⅔ cup/150 ml water.

■ Mix all the ingredients with a hand mixer until you have a smooth batter. Grease 12 individual muffin cups or 12 cups in a muffin pan and half-fill them with the batter.

■ Bake the muffins in the oven for 20 minutes. Insert a toothpick or skewer into the center of a muffin and if the toothpick comes out clean, the muffin is cooked. Let the muffins cool in their molds on a wire rack.

Khorasan is an ancient variety of wheat (see pages 28 and 146) and its good gluten properties make it especially suitable for bread making. Khorasan can be used in other batters, however (such as here in a sponge batter) and stand in for wheat or spelt flour.

Protein Bars with Quinoa and Apricots

Makes 5 large or 10 small bars

¼ cup/50 g red quinoa
¼ cup/50 g pitted dried dates
⅓ cup/50 g unsalted cashew nuts
½ cup/90 g dried apricots
⅔ cup/90 g raisins
1 tbsp cashew nut butter

■ Place the quinoa in a strainer and rinse under cold running water until the water runs clear, then cook in boiling water for 10 minutes. Strain through a strainer and drain well.

■ Place all the ingredients in a powerful food processor and whiz for a few seconds. If you only have a hand blender, soak the nuts in water for a few hours in advance.

■ Transfer the mixture to a small Dutch oven or casserole (approx. 7 x 4¼ inches/18 x 11 cm) and smooth the top. Alternatively, spread the mixture on a baking sheet lined with parchment paper. Chill in the refrigerator for at least for 1 hour and then cut into 5 large or 10 small bars. The bars will keep for about 3 days in the refrigerator.

These natural, vegan bars provide an extra portion of protein. With a protein content of 14 percent, quinoa, a pseudocereal, leaves all the other grain varieties standing. The bars are especially suitable for athletes, but they are also ideal for a snack on the go.

Apple and Cherry Crumble with Oat Flakes

Serves 2

2 small apples
7 oz/200 g
cherries
1 tbsp lemon
juice
4 tbsp whole
grain oat flakes
4 tbsp whole
grain spelt flour
2½ tbsp/40 g
butter or vegan
margarine
1 pinch ground
cinnamon
1 tbsp agave
syrup
Fat for greasing

■ Preheat the oven to 355°F/180°C or 320°F/160°C fan. Wash, quarter, and core the apples, and cut into bite-size pieces.

■ Wash, pit, and halve the cherries and mix them with the apples and lemon juice in a bowl. Combine the oat flakes and flour. Cut the butter or margarine into small pieces and rub into the oat flakes and flour. Add the cinnamon and agave syrup and combine to form a crumble.

■ Grease a Dutch oven, casserole, or heavy-bottom dish, then spoon in the apples and cherries, and arrange the crumble on top. Bake in the oven for 20 minutes.

You can use almost any kind of fruit variety in a crumble. I go for fruits that are in season, such as berries in summer, for example, and plums, apples, and pears in the fall.

Recipe Index

Acknowledgments

I would like to thank my parents, who not only showed me what it is to live a healthy lifestyle, but have also always stood behind me, providing unconditional support. My thanks are also due to my sister, who lent a hand from shopping to dishwashing and tested recipes with me for hours. I would also like to express my thanks to my husband—not only for believing in me, supporting me, and always being there for me, but also for being available as a test diner, evening after evening. I would also like to take this opportunity to thank the entire publishing team at Dort-Hagenhausen-Verlag and everyone who has helped in creating this book.

Abbreviations and quantities

1 oz = 1 ounce = 28 grams
1 lb = 1 pound = 16 ounces
1 cup = 8 ounces = 16 ounces
1 cup = 8 fluid ounces = 250 milliliters (liquids)
2 cups = 1 pint (liquids)
8 pints = 4 quarts = 1 gallon (liquids)
1g = 1 gram = 1/1000 kilogram
1kg = 1 kilogram = 1000 grams = 2¼ lb
1 l = 1 liter = 1000 milliliters (ml) = approx 34 fluid ounces
125 milliliters (ml) = approx. 8 tablespoons
1 tbsp = 1 level tablespoon = 15–20g (see below) =
15 milliliters (liquids)
1 tsp = 1 level teaspoon = 3–5g (see below) = 5ml (liquids)

Where measurements of dry ingredients are given in
spoons, this always refers to the prepared ingredient
as described in the wording immediately following, e.g.
1 tbsp chopped onions BUT: 1 onion, peeled and chopped.

Picture credits

Fotolia
pp. 4, 5

Hannah Frey
pp. 25, 41, 43, 46, 47, 49, 51, 54, 55, 57, 59, 61, 63, 65, 66,
67, 70, 71, 75, 76, 77, 79, 81, 82, 83, 85, 89, 93, 97, 99, 101,
105, 106, 109, 111, 113, 115, 117, 119, 120, 121, 124, 125, 127, 128,
130, 133, 134, 135, 137, 139, 143, 145, 148, 149, 151, 152, 153,
155, 156, 159, 161, 163, 164

Frank Nikisch
p. 7

Stockfood
pp. 2, 3, 8, 13, 19, 23, 27, 29, 31, 33, 35, 38, 44, 52, 68, 72,
86, 90, 102, 122, 140, 146

© Verlags- und Vertriebsgesellschaft Dort- Hagenhausen Verlag- GmbH & Co. KG, Munich
Original Title: *Clean Eating – natürlich kochen*
ISBN 978-3-86362-036-3

Editing of the original edition: Claudia Boss-Teichmann
Photography, design, composition: Christine Paxmann text · konzept · grafik, Munich

Disclaimer
The information and recipes printed in this book are provided to the best of our knowledge and
belief and from our own experience. However neither the author nor the publisher shall accept
liability for any damage whatsoever which may arise directly or indirectly from the use of this book.
It is advisable not to serve dishes that contain raw eggs to very young children, pregnant women,
elderly people, or to anyone weakened by serious illness. If in any doubt, consult your doctor.
Be sure that all the eggs you use are as fresh as possible.

© for this English edition: h.f.ullmann publishing GmbH
Translation from German: JMS Books llp in association with Malcolm Garrard
Typesetting: cbdesign

Overall responsibility for production: h.f.ullmann publishing GmbH, Potsdam, Germany

Printed in India, 2015

ISBN 978-3-8480-0866-7

10 9 8 7 6 5 4 3 2 1
X IX VIII VII VI V IV III II I

www.ullmann-publishing.com
newsletter@ullmann-publishing.com
facebook.com/ullmann.social